P9-EME-574

NORTH POLE

Doubleday Signal Books

NORTH POLE

The Story
of Robert E. Peary

TONY SIMON

Illustrated by Albert Orbaan

DOUBLEDAY & COMPANY, INC.
GARDEN CITY, NEW YORK

Library of Congress Catalog Card Number 60–11339
Copyright © 1961 by Doubleday & Company, Inc.
All Rights Reserved
Printed in the United States of America

CONTENTS

CHAPTER ONE

THE LURE OF THE FROZEN NORTH

"Let's skate across Casco Bay, Ned—it's frozen."

"Great idea, Bert!"

"We will explore Eagle Island and make believe that we have come to the aid of Sir John Franklin and his men in the Arctic."

"Right! I'll be Elisha Kane and you'll be Franklin——"

"No, I won't, Ned. I'm Kane, and you're Franklin. And today I try a daring dash across thin ice to pick up your trail."

Two teen-age boys were planning a day of adventure in the winter of 1870. They were Robert "Bert" Peary and Edward "Ned" Reynolds of Portland, Maine. Both liked to think and play that they were deep in the hidden frozen North.

And Bert Peary enjoyed—best of all—playing the part of his hero, Elisha Kent Kane, Arctic explorer.

Kane had been a young doctor in the United States Navy. In 1850 he signed up to join an American expedition off for the Canadian Arctic. The expedition hoped to find Sir John Franklin, a British explorer, and 128 of his men. All 129 had disappeared while trying to find a northern waterway from the Atlantic Ocean to the Pacific Ocean.

Not one man was found alive.

After returning home, Kane wrote a book called *Arctic Adventures*. It came out in 1856, the year Bert Peary was born. Kane's book was written in the form of a diary. To Bert, each day was more thrilling than the last. He and Ned Reynolds read *Arctic Adventures* together—and Bert couldn't put it down.

Often he read Kane's words aloud. They were so real to the lean, redheaded boy, he pictured himself exploring with Kane:

They were forever pushing northward.

"My mind has been made up from the first that

we are to force our way to the north as far as the weather will let us," wrote Kane. "If we can only reach the little isle ahead of us and hold there until the winds give us fairer prospect. Midnight! We did reach it—and just in time! But it is blowing a gale now and the ice is driving northward before it . . ."

They were forever in danger.

"I was awakened one evening from a sound sleep in my fox-skins, to discover that we had fairly lost our way," Kane reported. "A large iceberg had covered our track. We could not turn back. I ordered the boats hauled up and made a camp on the ice. It was truly frightening. We were deep in the bay, surrounded on all sides by huge icebergs and ice floes."

They were forever in search of food.

"With a wild yell the men seized the seal and bore it to safer ice," Kane wrote. "The men seemed half-crazed with hunger. They ran over the ice, crying and laughing and waving their knives. It was not five minutes before every man was sucking his bloody fingers or eating long strips of raw fat. . . . I killed today my first polar bear."

They were forever battling icy winds.

"We have had a rough night. The wind blew a gale from the northwest and the thermometer fell rapidly. The wind roared over the ice and everything about the ship froze. The wind is howling across the ice ridges. I reached the deck and the wind was there, blowing stiff, and the sails were puffing with it."

And there were moments of victory.

"In the midst of it all, our little weather-beaten ship ran up the first American flag that had been seen in the port of Proven."

Arctic explorer!

That was Bert Peary's fondest dream of himself. . . . He would brave freezing gales, drive Eskimo dogs forward, camp on floating ice. He would struggle in an open boat one day, battle a savage polar bear the next. Cold and hungry, bundled in furs, he would press on to save a lost party or to discover new land in the vast Arctic.

Bert Peary admired Arctic explorers for their great courage. Although tall and thin, Bert had no fear.

One winter afternoon at school an older boy, much heavier than Bert, hit him with a snowball. It knocked off Bert's new hat. As he picked it up, Bert saw the older boy run up to him.

"Hey, Skinny, don't wear your hat—or I'll knock it off again," the troublemaker warned.

Bert put on his hat without saying a word.

"Well, start walking, mama's little boy," said the bully, making another snowball.

Bert took two quick steps forward. His strong hands grabbed the older boy's throat. In the same motion, Bert tripped him, pushed his face into the snow, and sat on his back. The bully could not stir as Bert bounced his face in the snow.

Bert Peary was neither weak nor cowardly. All

11

muscle, he kept in trim. He could skate, play ball, wrestle, ride horseback, dive, swim, hike long distances.

He loved the outdoors—and had much of it indoors! Scattered around his room were stuffed birds, rock samples, mounted butterflies, snake skins, hawk nests, odd-shaped tree twigs.

Bert kept a careful record of everything he collected—when, where, and how he found it. Soon this record took the shape of his own diary.

In 1873 Peary was graduated from Portland High School. He won a scholarship in civil engineering and entered Bowdoin College. A top student, Peary still found time to take part in sports. He was good in the high jump, running broad jump, and hammer throw. His powerful strokes as an oarsman helped a Bowdoin crew win a cup.

One day in 1875 he entered a baseball throwing contest at Bowdoin. The idea was to see who could fling a ball the longest distance. Each man was to throw three times. Only his best try counted.

"Peary? He doesn't stand a chance! Not against ballplayers." That was what most people said who were watching the contest. Peary was the last man to try. He could win the contest by heaving the ball past 306 feet, the longest throw of the day.

A strong wind blew the ball to one side. It barely reached 290 feet. The second throw got to 300 feet.

There was still one chance left. He'd give it his all.

It reached 316 feet!

During his four years at Bowdoin, Peary studied hard. He was graduated in 1877 with top honors in civil engineering.

After graduation, Peary became a town surveyor at Fryeburg, Maine. His job was to make surveys and maps of property lines in and around the town.

Two years dragged by. Peary was not content. Something seemed to be missing in his life. He had hoped to see more of the world than Fryeburg.

Peary felt a great need for change. But where—and how? Suddenly he thought of a United States poster he had seen in town. He ran to the post office to read the poster tacked on a wall.

The poster announced four job openings in the United States Coast and Geodetic Survey. Place: Washington, D.C. . . . Salary: $10 a week.

Peary sent in samples of his maps and surveys—and landed one of the jobs. At first he liked the work.

Soon, however, Peary found himself unhappy again. No, this was not quite the job he had wanted. He dreamed of a life of action . . . an explorer's life . . . a life of adventure.

A chance for change came in 1881. The Civil Engineering Corps of the United States Navy wanted men. Peary decided to prepare for the stiff test.

For ten days he locked himself in his room, studying twenty hours a day. He left the room only to eat.

More than 200 men took the test with Peary. Peary was sure he had not done well.

"I do not know the answers to many of your questions," he told the examiners.

Much to his surprise, one of them said: "Perhaps so—but you've made a good showing. We can see you're a man who will keep at a job until you finish it. That's the kind of men the U. S. Navy needs."

Only Peary and three other men passed the exams. On October 26, 1881, Peary became a lieutenant in the United States Navy.

He was delighted! With the Navy he'd get the chance to travel—perhaps to the four corners of the world. One day Peary was asked to see the Navy's chief engineer, Aniceto G. Menocal. "Lieutenant Peary," said the chief, "we have some work for you at Key West, Florida. You are to inspect a pier that the Navy is having built there. The builder isn't doing a good job. And his price is much too high. We would like a report from you. Tell us if the pier can be built, and the cost."

"I have one question, sir," said Peary. "What is the builder's price?"

"Thirty thousand dollars."

Peary left for Key West immediately. He spent days drawing up plans for the pier. At the pier site, he would often dive deep underwater to see for himself what the Key West bottom looked like. After several weeks, he finished his plans and wrote to the Navy.

Peary said the pier could be built—for much less than twenty thousand dollars.

Navy engineers were surprised.

"Peary is out of his mind," they told Menocal. "He'll never build a pier at Key West at that low price." The chief engineer smiled.

"Maybe you're right, but let's give him a chance."

Work on the pier began—and went along well. Then one morning as Peary left for the pier he felt dizzy. He had chills and fever at the same time. His muscles ached. A doctor ordered him to bed at once.

"You have yellow fever, Lieutenant," said the doctor. "Get in bed—and stay there."

"But the pier!" cried Peary. "The crew depends on me to show them just what's to be done."

The doctor refused to give in. He kept Peary in his room. Work on the pier stopped—but not for long. After a few days of rest and care, Peary improved. He would not remain idle in bed.

Peary hired a wheel chair. Early every morning he wheeled himself down to the pier with his plans for the work crews. The men, moved by his will power, worked harder than ever. They built the pier exactly as Peary had planned it.

The cost was $6,000—saving the Navy nearly $25,000!

When Peary returned home, Chief Engineer Menocal greeted him with a pleasant surprise.

"We are all proud of your work," said Menocal. "You have earned a promotion. Good luck on being first engineer of my staff!"

This news thrilled Peary. He had heard that Menocal was about to lead an expedition to the jungles of Nicaragua.

The Menocal expedition was to find a route for a ship canal through Nicaragua's jungles. The canal would link the Atlantic and Pacific Oceans.

The expedition left for Nicaragua by ship on December 20, 1884. One afternoon a few weeks later, the ship neared the Bahamas, a group of islands south of Florida. Peary, strolling on deck, was curious to see one island—San Salvador. Here was the very first shore that Columbus had seen in the New World.

As San Salvador came into view, Peary thought of Columbus. "The fame of Columbus will be equaled only by the man who stands at the top of the world—the discoverer of the North Pole," Peary wrote. For the moment, Peary did not know why he should think of the Arctic while on a trip to the tropics.

Was it the lure of the frozen North?

Did the names San Salvador and Columbus remind Peary of his own dreams of exploring?

For the next four months Peary had no time to think of the Arctic. He and a small party of men cut their way through a tangled jungle to open a ship canal route. They struggled against heat, mosquitoes, thirst, and hunger.

Peary worked far into each night designing locks for the canal. Then, without warning, work on the plan was called off. Peary, greatly disappointed, was ordered back to Washington.

It was then that he reached a turning point in his life. One evening in the fall of 1885 Peary visited a bookstore in Washington. Under a stack of books he found an old pamphlet written by a Swedish explorer. Peary bought the pamphlet and finished it that night. It described the Swede's journeys across blizzard-battered areas of Greenland deep in the frozen North.

So little is known about Greenland, thought Peary. Is it an island? Does it reach as far north as the North Pole? Will anyone ever cross from Greenland's west coast to its east coast? How high are its mountains?

How useful an expedition would be. A man could really test his skill there as an Arctic explorer. And he might someday get as far as the North Pole!

That evening Peary made up his mind. He would explore Greenland.

CHAPTER TWO

OFF TO GREENLAND

For months Peary read everything he could find on Greenland. Books by Arctic explorers piled up in his Washington room. He filled his notebooks with facts and drawings useful for Arctic travel.

On the walls were large maps he had made showing routes for crossing Greenland. Much of this was guesswork. No one—not even the Eskimos—knew Greenland's exact boundaries.

Although a colony of Denmark, Greenland was little known to the world. As he studied his maps, Peary wished he knew the answer to this question:

Does the northern part of Greenland reach as far as the North Pole?

Early in 1886 Peary asked the Navy for time off.

"How long do you plan to be away, Lieutenant?" asked Chief Engineer Menocal.

"About six months, sir."

"Good. We may be sent to Nicaragua next year. And I want you along."

The Navy agreed to give Peary a six-month leave. Next, he visited his mother in Maine. Peary spent hours talking about Greenland.

"But why go there?" asked Mrs. Peary.

"No one has really explored Greenland, Mother. No one knows how far north it reaches. And hardly anything is known about the east coast."

"Won't the trip be dangerous?"

"I am prepared," answered Peary. "I have read much on Greenland and Arctic travel. Think of exploring an area where no one has ever set foot!"

Mrs. Peary saw that nothing would stop him.

Peary bought passage on the *Eagle*, an Arctic-bound whaling boat. She sailed from northern Canada's Cape Breton Island late in May 1886. The sturdy ship sped across the icy North Atlantic. Then she slammed her way up ice-clogged Davis Strait between Greenland and Canada's Baffin Island.

For Peary this voyage was "a never-to-be-forgotten memory."

Heavy gales swept down on the *Eagle*. During

most of the trip, Peary roamed the deck. It was during this trip that he caught the Arctic fever from which he never recovered.

Peary thrilled to "the ship's rolling and pitching, as if mad, the decks awash with water, and the foam and spray driving over the rail and across . . . a blinding drift of snow . . ."

Huge pieces of ice closed in on the *Eagle* as she passed Cumberland Sound off Baffin Island.

Peary, standing near the wheel, turned to Captain Arthur Jackman.

"How can we ever break through this ice?"

"You've just told me."

"I've what?"

"You've answered your own question!"

"I don't understand."

Captain Jackman laughed to see Peary so puzzled.

"We will *break* through the ice, by rolling the *Eagle* from side to side," he explained. "All of the crew will run to one side of the ship. Under their weight, she'll crush the ice directly below. With her engines at full speed, she'll work forward a bit. Then the crew will run to the other side of the deck. As the weight changes, she'll again smash the ice——"

"—And again move ahead!" broke in Peary. "Wonderful!"

For nearly twenty-four hours the *Eagle*, swaying from side to side, shattered the ice. With Peary joining in, the men raced back and forth across the deck.

Slowly the powerful engines drove the *Eagle* out of the ice trap. "A day later, and we would not have escaped," wrote Peary.

Peary wasted no time getting to work when he reached Greenland's west coast. His first problem: Peary spoke no Danish, and no one he met spoke English. His answer: He used his hands in "sign language" or he made drawings.

Peary showed a Danish official drawings of two sledges he had designed. The official asked Eskimos to help Peary build them.

To explore Greenland, shaped like a turtle's back, Peary first had to climb a steep slope rising from the west coast. The slope reached up to Greenland's rugged plateau. It is a huge stretch of ice, hardened after great storms of centuries, that sits higher than the coastal areas. Greenland's ice plateau, nearly three times the size of Texas, looms thousands of feet above sea level. The Danish official rounded up a team of eight Eskimos to guide Peary. Along with them came young Christian Maigaard. He was the Danish manager of the Eskimos' settlement.

Maigaard admired Peary for his pluck in coming to Greenland alone. Neither man could speak the other's language. Both, however, understood the spirit of adventure.

In sign language Peary explained his plan. He wished to find a place along the coastal mountains where he could climb to the plateau. From there he hoped to move inland across the ice.

Maigaard had the Eskimos load Peary's sledges and equipment in small boats. Then the party rowed swiftly to an inlet.

In four days—with no dogs to help them—the men pulled the heavy sledges up to the western edge of the sparkling plateau of ice. They were now breathing sharp Arctic air 2,000 feet above the sea.

Before them stretched Greenland's rising inland ice. The bright sun's glare on the clean ice blinded Peary. He put on his dark glasses to study the brilliant scene—bright white ice and bright blue sky.

Maigaard motioned to show that from here the ice plateau slanted to 10,000 feet above sea level. In sign language the two men planned their next move:

PEARY: Let's travel alone across the ice.

MAIGAARD: You and me? Alone?

PEARY: We can travel faster and farther alone. Our supplies will last longer.

MAIGAARD: It will be hard work without the Eskimos to help us pull the sledges.

PEARY: We are strong enough. We can do it.

MAIGAARD: You're right! I will have the Eskimos set up camp. They'll wait here until we return.

PEARY: Good! Let's move out at once.

Dragging the sledges, the two men started out. In many places wide cracks had ripped open the ice. Some were hundreds of feet deep. They marched around the cracks, or across them on newly formed bridges of ice that covered the cracks.

When the explorers reached 3,000 feet a coming

snowstorm darkened the sky. Strong winds howled across the gray plateau.

Peary motioned to Maigaard to help him turn each sledge on its side. They pushed the sledges together to form a "V." Then they threw a large piece of canvas over the sides.

For two days the trapped explorers crowded behind the sledges while gale winds shrieked by.

They pressed forward again when the storm died. That same morning Peary nearly lost his life. Observing the ice ahead, he did not see a crack, hidden by fresh snow, under his feet.

Suddenly he found himself dropping into the ice. Somehow he managed to hold his body against the sides of the crack. He broke his fall. Carefully he pulled himself out of the crack. Seconds later, the sides of the crack crumbled and fell in.

Peary had learned a rule about the Arctic he was not to forget:

Never trust ice. Be sure it can hold your weight.

Soon after, another storm arose. "We advanced with goggles on, hoods pulled up, and heads down," wrote Peary. The wind blew harder. At times the whirling snow—a cloud of white darkness—blotted out the sun. For another week they continued their slow advance.

One morning Maigaard motioned to Peary:

Maigaard (pointing to sledges): Our supplies are running low.

PEARY: I think we've gone as far as we can.

MAIGAARD: No one has ever marched this far across Greenland.

PEARY (disappointed): But we've still such a long way to reach the east coast.

MAIGAARD: We had better go one way—west —back to camp—before it's too late!

PEARY (checking the sledges): You are right. We have food left for only six days.

Food for six days—and they had been traveling twenty days. They must return to camp at a much faster pace.

Peary knew from his Arctic reading that sledges

could be turned into a sailboat. He and Maigaard lashed the sledges side by side. Then they tied a canvas sail to a long upright pole put up between the sledges. For a rudder, Peary fastened a large hatchet to the back of one sledge.

Off they sailed, streaking down the frozen slopes "with a breathless rush." The return trip was all downhill with strong winds at their backs.

They were stopped only by cracks in the ice. To cross, they pushed the sledges over the crack until the front ends rested on the opposite side. Peary jumped across the crack to pull the sledges, while Maigaard pushed them. Then Maigaard jumped across and they continued toward camp.

Both men were glad to see the camp come into sight. About fifty yards in front of it stretched a deep, long crack in the ice. Peary leaped over the crack, and the "push-pull" crossing began. The front half of the sledges was resting on Peary's side of the crack—when Maigaard slipped.

As he fell into the crack, he grabbed the back end of the sledges. Up shot the front ends! They nearly tore out of Peary's strong hands. With all his strength, he pulled down on the front ends.

The sledges moved like a seesaw—at the very edge of the crack.

Slowly Peary brought down the front. This raised the back ends and Maigaard. Quickly Peary pulled

the sledges along the ice. Maigaard, as white as snow, scrambled out of the crack.

For two days they rested at the camp, Peary with "burning eyes and cracked and blistered face."

When they reached the west coast, he said good-by to Maigaard. The Dane was as sorry to see Peary leave as Peary was sorry to go.

"But I will come back someday," he let Maigaard know. "There are many things I want to find out about Greenland."

Peary left Greenland satisfied with the results of his short expedition:

He now knew how to travel across Arctic ice.

He had mastered some of the frozen North's hidden secrets.

He had, with Maigaard, pushed deeper into Greenland than any man.

And no one had climbed higher on the ice plateau than Peary.

The young explorer was drawn more than ever to the Arctic. Its great white spaces lured him. Now he had found his life's work: Arctic explorer.

Someday, in fact, he might be the first man to cross Greenland. After that . . . he might reach the top of the world . . . the North Pole.

CHAPTER THREE

EXPEDITION LEADER

For weeks the challenge of Greenland's open ice was fresh in Peary's mind. He wrote a report on his trip for the American Geographical Society in 1886.

He would like nothing better than to have the Navy or a private group to send him back to Greenland—as the leader of an expedition. Peary's hopes soared when his Greenland report came out. Then they dropped as quickly as pin-struck balloons.

No one took him seriously.

Scientists scoffed: "Who is this unknown Peary to write about Greenland and the Arctic?"

Navy officers grumbled: "Our men should have more important things to do than go on a wild goose chase to Greenland."

Taxpayers complained: "Arctic trips cost too much. Let's not have the Government spending our money so easily."

All talk of an American expedition ended. Peary, disappointed, returned to his Navy duties. For the time being he would forget about Greenland. In the spring of 1887, Chief Engineer Menocal called Peary.

"Work on the Nicaraguan canal is about to start again. You are to be in charge of the survey crews."

With Peary that summer went Matt Henson, a young Negro, who was to serve as the lieutenant's all-around man.

Peary spent seven months in Nicaragua in command of 150 men. He learned to become a leader, and he led men well. They hacked out mile after mile of the canal route in a steaming jungle.

In the spring of 1888, Peary and Henson returned to Washington. Once again Peary had time to think of his favorite plan—exploring Greenland.

The Arctic, however, wasn't all that Peary had on his mind. He had fallen in love with Josephine Diebitsch, the daughter of a professor in Washington. Josephine was pretty, young, bright. Peary enjoyed her lively jokes and quick smile. How delighted he was that she never tired of his long talks on Greenland or his plans to cross it.

"Do you know, Bert," she would tease him, "it is an hour since you told me what I long to hear."

"That I love you?"

"Heavens, no! That you will be first man to cross Greenland!"

"And I will, too, Jo."

They were married on August 11, 1888.

Soon after, Peary was sent to New York City. He and Josephine lived there in a cozy one-room apart-

ment. For about two months, life was perfect. Then one fall evening Peary came home unhappy.

"What's wrong, Bert?" asked Josephine. "Tell me, what is it?"

Peary turned to her.

"Jo, I'm too late," he said. "Nansen has crossed Greenland."

Peary was referring to Fridtjof Nansen, a great Arctic explorer from Norway. News flashes reported that he had crossed southern Greenland's ice plateau from the east coast to the west coast.

This was a most remarkable trip. A whaling boat had dropped off Nansen's party of six men along the

east coast. Once the men started across Greenland,
there was no turning back. They would have to
reach the west coast—or die.

Nansen had covered a 300-mile route much like
one of three that Peary hoped to take.

For days Peary was angry. Then he stopped feeling sorry for himself. He began to praise Nansen and
his brave men for doing a magnificent job. Yet, as he
told Josephine, there was still much to do in Greenland—and he would do it.

"Nansen deserves all the honor in the world,"
Peary said to Josephine one evening, while mapping
out Nansen's journey. "Yet his expedition tells

nothing of northern Greenland. Suppose it goes far to the north, to the Pole itself. By sledging over northern Greenland—I could reach the Pole!"

"Bert," asked Josephine, "why is this so important to you?"

"I don't know exactly. One reason, I suppose, is because no one has ever been there. Think of standing at the very top of the world!

"There are other reasons, too," he went on. "Whoever reaches the Pole will help science. Man will know that much more about the Earth. The discovery of the Pole will be a great event in history. It's something I'd be proud to have an American do."

Peary showed Josephine his wall map.

"Is northern Greenland a likely starting point for a dash to the Pole? I'd like to find out."

"How? Where do you intend going?"

"Here—to Whale Sound—by ship. Then I would head northeast by dog team, as far as I could go."

Peary had more than enough ideas and plans. What he now needed was money. He began to make speeches before scientific groups. He hammered on three points:

Greenland's northern border is not known.

It could pave the way to the North Pole.

America has a chance to lead the world in exploring the Arctic.

For nearly three years Peary spoke to scientists, wrote letters to important people, outlined his expedition plans. During this time he was assigned to a Navy yard in Philadelphia. He found a job on his staff for Matt Henson.

In 1891 the tide began to turn as people took notice of Peary's efforts and plans. Top United States scientists got behind him.

They agreed to provide money for an expedition to Greenland. Cheered by this backing—nearly $10,000 worth—Peary wrote to the Navy:

"I respectfully request leave of absence for eighteen months from May 1, 1891. . . . This is an age of truth seeking and truth getting, and no fact, however remote it may appear . . . is valueless."

The Navy approved a leave of eighteen months for Peary.

He immediately set to work rounding up a team of five men. Along with Matt Henson were two scientists, a doctor, and a young Norwegian, Eivind Astrup. He was a champion skier, hardened to the cold weather of the far north.

Peary couldn't wait to get started. Then, one evening in the spring of 1891 Josephine surprised him.

"Bert," she said, "I am coming along with you."

"With me? To Greenland?"

"Yes."

"Are you serious?"

"Yes. I am young and strong and healthy. And I *am* your wife."

"But what will people say——" began Peary.

35

"Let them say what they will. I want to be with you. Danish women and Eskimo women live in Greenland. Why not I?"

It would not help to argue. Josephine was aboard the expedition ship, the *Kite*, when Peary sailed for Greenland on June 6, 1891.

A month later the *Kite* moved deep into the Arctic off Greenland's west coast. At Melville Bay, the ship reached ice-clogged waters. Peary was on deck standing next to the wheel when a huge cake of ice crashed into the rudder. The sudden blow tore the wheel loose from the wheelsman's hand. Swinging furiously back, the wheel hit Peary and snapped two bones above his right ankle.

In great pain, he was carried to his cabin, where the doctor set the broken leg.

"Will he be all right, doctor?" asked Josephine.

"I'm sure he will. But I'm afraid this ends the expedition. He won't be able to walk for months."

"Then we should turn back without delay," said Josephine.

"NO!" Peary shouted. "We are not going back."

"If you're not careful, you may cripple yourself for life," warned the doctor. "Return home before it's too late."

"NO!" Peary raised himself on one elbow. "Scientists are behind me. I can't let them down. It will take more than a broken leg to stop me now."

Josephine began to nurse her husband back to

health. She admired his spunk. Once when pain stabbed at his leg, Josephine cried, "Tell me where it hurts most! What can I do to help?"

And Peary answered with a weak smile, "You might pack my leg in ice, hold it up—and let everyone take shots at it!"

Two weeks later the *Kite* sailed into Whale Sound, far up Greenland's western coast. The men prepared to leave the ship one morning to start building a winter camp. Peary asked to be brought ashore.

"The steady rocking of the ship bothers me," he explained to Josephine. "I'd like to live in a tent until the men finish the house."

"If you do go ashore, I am going with you," said Josephine.

On July 28, 1891, the doctor lashed Peary to a board to keep his broken leg from moving. The crew carried him to shore, then put up his tent. The men started to build a wooden house at the foot of cliffs.

The next morning the men returned from the ship to work on the house and to set up the rest of the camp. To keep busy, Peary directed their work from his chair. For five weeks he could not take a step. But by mid-August he got around with crutches.

Every day his leg felt a little stronger. He was able to join the men on hunting trips. They went out after reindeer, walrus, seal, bears. The meats were cut up and stored away for the long Arctic winter.

One day the men decided to hunt for walrus from

one of their small boats. Peary asked Josephine to come along. Soon the men came upon a school of walrus and opened fire. But instead of swimming away, the walrus turned and charged. They kept smashing against the boat, hoping to turn it over. For an hour Josephine, sitting next to Peary, loaded the guns for the men until they drove off the walrus.

"A scene I shall not easily forget," wrote Peary, "is Josephine calmly reloading our guns while all around the boat angry walrus poked their heads and tusks at us."

In October the days and the hunting trips grew shorter and shorter. Cold weather set in as strong winds whipped down from the north. Ice began to form on the sea, and the first snow fell.

By November the sun had all but disappeared from the sky. Daylight hours were hazy, nights pitch black except for two weeks when the moon hung low in the sparkling sky. Then bright silvery light streamed across the fresh snow.

But when storms blew in, or when the sky clouded over, all turned to darkness and a shadow settled on the land both day and night.

In December Peary and Matt Henson made friends with Eskimos who visited the camp. Peary was pleased to have them. "We need dogs and furs," he explained to Matt. "And we can learn much from the Eskimos about putting up igloos, building sledges, keeping food, making fur clothing, training dogs."

"And hunting," put in Matt. "Do you know that the Eskimos use *nets* to catch birds that fly too close to the ground after food?"

Peary told the expedition that it would spend the rest of the winter building sledges and preparing for the trip. "When spring comes, we'll head northeast on sledges. By then Matt and I will know how to handle the dogs. We'll get them from the Eskimos."

More and more Eskimos, returning from their hunting grounds, stopped at the camp. They brought with them dogs, furs, walrus, and seal meat. The Eskimos traded with Peary for guns, shells, tea, hatchets, beads, bracelets, tin cups, and tin plates.

Soon the temperature dropped to below zero, and icy winds cut through the camp. Peary and Josephine and the men looked forward to the good cheer of Christmas. On Christmas Day they invited the neighboring Eskimos to camp for a friendly visit. Peary, now in good health, joined in the fun. To test his healed leg, he entered a snowshoe race—and won!

Peary paid honor to an American flag in the dining room with these words: "To the flag over us—the brightest that waves—I offer the hope that our little party may add to its lustre."

Later Peary and Josephine exchanged Christmas gifts. He gave her two hairpins carved from walrus tusks. She gave him a hand-sewn blue and white flag made of a silk handkerchief and part of a silk dress.

On the white field was a blue "P" for Peary, on a blue field a white star to represent the North Star.

Peary was moved by Josephine's thoughtful gift. "Your flag will fly from my sledge when I cross northern Greenland next spring."

And one day, he thought, an American flag will fly at the North Pole.

CHAPTER FOUR

ARCTIC ADVENTURES

IN JANUARY the temperature dropped to twenty degrees below zero. A heavy snowfall half buried the wooden house. Inside, gathered around kerosene lamps, Peary and the men prepared for the trip across northern Greenland.

Peary designed winter clothes and sleeping bags much like those used by the Eskimos. His men cut, stretched, and dried their animal skins. Peary then called in Eskimo women to sew for the men.

"How can they ever sew these skins?" asked Josephine. "Each skin is as hard as a rock."

The Eskimo women folded a skin so that the fur was on the inside. Then inch by inch they *chewed* the skin back and forth along the edge until it was soft enough to push a needle through.

They made bearskin pants, hareskin stockings, sealskin boots, deerskin mittens, and fur coats with fur hoods. An Arctic outfit designed by Peary weighed twelve pounds. This was about half the weight of an Eskimo outfit—yet was just as warm.

"If you want to cover long distances in the Arctic you have to travel lightly," Peary told the men.

They spent much time preparing a special food, called pemmican, for the coming trip. Peary's pemmican was a kind of Arctic hamburger—chopped walrus, whale fat, spices, sugar.

"We'll use pemmican only in emergencies, when there's nothing else to eat," Peary told the men.

"It doesn't taste good," said Eivind Astrup, nibbling at a piece.

"Maybe so," Peary said. "But that's because you're not hungry now. You'd eat pemmican if you had nothing else. And it would keep you alive."

"How much pemmican would a man get in one day?" asked Matt Henson.

"About a pound," Peary answered. "He'll also have a pound of dried biscuit, some tea, and a little sugar. But we'll always be on the lookout for fresh food—musk oxen, hares, birds, bears, fish. If we don't find any, we'll eat pemmican and biscuits."

The sledges Peary designed were thirteen feet long, several feet larger than those used by the Eskimos. Yet Peary's sledges were lighter. By using fewer pieces of wood, Peary cut the weight of a sledge from 125 pounds to under 50 pounds.

"Every pound we snip off a sledge means an extra pound of food we can take along," Peary told Matt Henson, who built the sledges.

Matt Henson became an expert in training dog

teams. With Peary, he quickly learned the Eskimo language. Matt, kind and friendly, enjoyed speaking with the Eskimos. They, in turn, were eager to show him all they knew about handling dogs.

"The most important thing," Henson explained to the men, "is to aim a command right at the lead dog. He's the best fighter among the dogs. They know it and fear him. The dogs will follow him and do whatever he does. You have to let your lead dog know what you want done."

"But how do we aim a command at *one* dog, when there are several pulling a sledge?"

"You crack your whip so that it snaps right at the tip of the lead dog's ear—without hitting it," Matt said. "At the exact same time you shout your command. For example, 'HUK! HUK!' is my order for the dogs to start."

"And when you want them to stop?"

"I crack the whip at the lead dog's ear and yell, 'AYE! AYE!'"

Peary's plan was to start moving north as soon as daylight returned in February.

"We'll be able to see what we're doing," he explained to Josephine. "The worst part of winter will be over in February, yet it will be cold enough to keep firm ice under our sledges."

"I thought Greenland's plateau is so high and so cold that it has ice all year round," said Josephine.

"That's true," said Peary, "but from the maps I've

made, I don't believe Greenland's northern coast is more than 500 miles away. Suppose it's much less than that—and we reach the Arctic Ocean."

"You'll continue across the ocean, if it's still frozen."

"That is right," said Peary. "In *winter* the Arctic Ocean is frozen thick. I want to get there before April or May, while the ice is still hard. In late spring and summer the ice begins to melt. It cracks and sways and opens up like this."

Peary slowly spread his fingers wide to show how melting ice splits. "No one can get far crossing the Arctic Ocean once warm weather arrives."

In February the deep blue sky began to show a pale glow. This soft light came from the sun, which had dipped out of sight in late fall. Now each day brought thin rays of golden light to the dark sky. Daylight was returning.

On February 14, 1892, Peary decided to climb to a point high on the ice plateau. The time had come to begin moving supplies from the base camp up to the plateau for the start of the northern trip.

With Peary on this test march were Eivind Astrup and Dr. Frederick A. Cook. After a steep climb, they reached 2,000 feet.

Sharp winds whirled about in forty below zero temperature. To protect themselves, the men built a small shelter made of ice blocks.

The box-shaped house was nine feet long, six feet

wide, three feet high. Its flat roof, made of thin ice blocks, rested on Astrup's skis. The skis were laid out from wall to wall.

After a meal of pemmican, biscuits, and tea, the men tried to get some sleep. They spread out their deerskin sleeping bags inside the small snowhouse. It was so crowded that the men pushed their clothing outside, weighing it down under their snowshoes. Then each man—wearing only his heavy underwear—crawled into his sleeping bag.

Just before he fell asleep, Peary reached outside for his hand shovel. A few hours later, he awoke with snow blowing into his face. The strong wind had ripped away a corner of the house where the roof and wall met.

Snow, piling on the men, was burying them alive!

Peary wiggled free. He woke Dr. Cook and helped him free his arms. But Astrup, curled in a corner, was pinned down under a mountain of snow. He could hardly breathe. A wall of piled-up snow blocked Peary from reaching Astrup, but Cook could get to him.

"Push the snow away from his face so that he gets some air," Peary shouted to Cook. "I'll get to him from the outside."

"Hurry!" Cook answered.

Peary pushed up hard against one of the roof skis. He opened a hole with his shovel. Then, sleeping bag and all, he tumbled out of the snowhouse.

The wind slammed him against the side of the

snowhouse. Crawling slowly, he worked his way to the corner where Astrup lay trapped. With powerful strokes of his shovel, Peary ripped a hole out of the corner. He freed Astrup and pulled him out. Cook crawled out behind Astrup. All three huddled against the side of the house, which soon became packed with the gale-blown snow.

"We could not have stood up before such a gale if we had tried," Peary wrote. "All we could do was to crouch, half sitting, with our backs to the storm. . . . We sat there hour after hour."

Hail rattled down on the men shivering in their sleeping bags. The bags began to freeze and stiffen as the ice stuck fast.

"Keep twisting and turning from side to side," Peary shouted above the storm. "Shake off the ice. If you don't keep moving, you'll be frozen solid inside a bag of ice."

For hours he kept reminding Cook and Astrup to move, and they did. After the storm ended, all three men took turns digging out their clothing.

As the men headed back to camp, Peary told them he had now learned two new rules about Arctic travel.

"Always build a rounded igloo for shelter—not one with straight walls. Even the strongest winds slide over a rounded igloo and can't open it."

"And the other rule?" asked Cook.

"Always keep clothing and food within reach, even if that means *stuffing* it inside your sleeping bag."

As the men reached camp that morning in mid-February, sunlight flooded the sky. Welcome daylight, bright and cheerful, was at hand. The men stopped to watch the blazing sun lift into the sky.

From February until May, the men moved supplies by dog team from the base camp to an advance "igloo base." It was built at the foot of the high ice plateau. Peary's idea was to store as much food as close to the ice field as they could get. By May they had moved enough food to last for a round trip of about 1,200 miles.

On May 4, 1892, Peary said good-by to Josephine. She was worried about him. Was his foot healed? Was he healthy enough for a long journey?

"I feel fine," Peary told his wife. "And I have your silk flag for good luck!"

Josephine's flag was tied to the end of a tall bamboo pole. Peary could carry the pole while walking and testing ice ahead of the sledges. Or, when riding, he could fasten the pole to the front of his lead sledge.

With Peary in the lead the men started out: Henson, Astrup, Cook, and Langdon Gibson, one of the expedition's scientists.

Each man had his own sledge, pulled by four dogs. As the men and dogs climbed the steep plateau, raging winds blew icy clouds of snow into their faces. During the next few days, the temperature dropped sharply. Matt Henson's heel became so badly frozen he could hardly stand.

Peary ordered Henson back to camp for medical care and rest: "Your health comes first—there will be other trips for you."

Henson returned with one dog, and the expedition pushed north. They began to climb—2,500 feet . . . 3,000 feet . . . 3,500 feet—and to move deeper into the ice field—10 miles . . . 40 miles . . . 85 miles . . . 130 miles.

Each day the going grew worse as icy winds tore across the plateau. Three of the dogs went mad and died. A sudden blizzard pinned the men down for forty-eight hours.

The delays and slow travel worried Peary. "We are eating up our food, yet we're not covering enough ground," he told the men.

"But we eat only two meals a day—and skimpy ones," they protested. "What more can we do?"

"I have one answer," said Peary. "Two of you must return to camp. One will come with me."

All three men asked to stay. Peary made up his mind quickly—Astrup. He was young and hardy.

On May 24, Cook and Gibson left for camp with two dogs. Peary and Astrup, with fourteen dogs, turned north. The great "White March" began toward unknown northern Greenland.

Peary led the way, marching about twenty feet in front of Astrup and the dogs. As he checked the ice, Peary used Josephine's flag to signal directions to Astrup. The blue flag served as a landmark in the blinding glare of the sun-struck ice field.

"Many times I found myself traveling in gray space," wrote Peary. "I could feel the snow under me but was unable to see it. There was no sun, no sky, no horizon, nothing my eyes could rest upon!"

Josephine's flag comforted Peary. It was good to see something else that was real in the cold gray "nothingness."

Each day was almost like the one before—icy winds, flashing glare, long marches in the snow. Each meal was much the same—pemmican, powdered pea soup, biscuits, hot tea.

The dogs, hungry for fresh food, became mean-tempered. They snapped and growled all the time. At night they often fought among themselves. The dogs

would tangle their harness straps so badly that Peary and Astrup lost hours trying to untangle them.

One day two dogs, fighting and chasing each other, suddenly disappeared! They had fallen into a deep crack. One end of the tangled harness caught on a jagged piece of ice. Peary raced to the crack, grabbed the strap, and hung onto it. Then he and Astrup pulled up the dogs—still snapping at each other.

"We better find fresh meat—or we'll have no dogs left," Peary said.

"But where?" asked Astrup.

Peary had no answer.

By mid-June his broken leg began to swell and ache under the strain. He and Astrup had now traveled nearly 500 miles, and climbed to 8,000 feet. Yet the end of the ice plateau was not in sight. Nor was there any sign of game for fresh food.

For two weeks more they pushed across the ice. On June 26 Peary saw low coastal mountains in the distance. The ice plateau now sloped downward, and patches of land appeared on it. All this meant they were nearing Greenland's northern coast, which was free of ice and snow in summer.

Peary started down the sloping plateau eager to see what lay ahead. On July 1 the men and dogs entered a barren, rocky valley. Leaving the sledges behind, the men and dogs moved across the valley. Suddenly Peary stopped and dropped to his knees.

"What's wrong?" asked Astrup.

"Look! Musk ox tracks!"

Peary knew that the shaggy musk ox, a grazing cattle-like animal, had beef-like meat.

"If we can shoot one or two we'll have all the fresh meat that *all* of us can eat," Peary said.

He told Astrup to hold the dogs behind so that the musk ox would not be frightened off. Peary then moved ahead quietly. Several hundred yards away, he saw two of the woolly animals.

Before they could charge or escape, Peary ran forward. He took aim and fired at the nearest musk ox, bringing it down with two shots. Quickly he turned and got the second animal with one shot.

For two days Peary, Astrup, and the dogs feasted on musk ox steaks.

On July 4 Peary and Astrup climbed out of the valley to the top of a 4,000-foot hill covered with rocks. They were now standing at the edge of a wall-like cliff. Spread out below to the northeast was a bay opening into the Arctic Ocean. Huge icebergs stuck out from its frozen waters.

"It was almost impossible for us to believe that we were standing upon the northern shore of Greenland," wrote Peary. From this high view, it seemed likely to him that Greenland was *not* a continent.

Greenland was an island. This was one of Peary's gifts to geography.

Then he piled big stones in one high heap as proof that he had stood at Greenland's northern coast. Inside the stones he put a tightly-corked bottle. It contained papers telling of the trip across Greenland.

Peary set one end of a long pole into the top of the stones. From the pole flew three flags. Two were American flags belonging to scientific societies that had backed Peary. The third was Josephine's blue and white flag, Peary's "beacon" across Greenland.

On July 8 they headed south for home. After climbing back up to the ice plateau, they moved rapidly across the ice.

Once a sudden blizzard stopped them in their tracks. For two days and two nights Peary and Astrup lay under canvas sheets "listening to the howling of the storms and shrieking of the wind rushing by." But after that they had an easy march.

On August 6, 1892, the long "White March" ended—after 1,300 miles. Peary could not wait to greet Josephine, whom he had not seen for three months. "He rattled at my door, calling to me to open it," Josephine wrote. "But I seemed to be paralyzed. He forced it open and stood before me . . . safe at last. I had only one fear: that I might wake up and find this all a dream."

CHAPTER FIVE

ARCTIC HARDSHIPS

PEARY returned to the United States in the fall of 1892. Newspaper stories of his "White March" across northern Greenland thrilled millions of Americans.

Scientists of many lands praised Peary for his 1,300-mile sledge trip over land never explored before. His maps showed that he had crossed Greenland 1,000 miles *north* of Nansen's 300-mile trip of 1888.

This warm welcome stirred Peary. He immediately outlined another trip to Greenland.

The Navy gave Peary a three-year leave. Money, however, again became a problem, for he hoped to return to Greenland the following spring. This meant he had about six months to raise $80,000 for a ship, supplies, tools, equipment.

"Can't scientific societies help you?" asked Josephine. "Surely they believe in you and in your work."

"They do, but they have no money to spare."

How could he raise $80,000 in six months? Everyone seemed so interested in his travels yet money was so hard to get. People in the streets stopped him to ask questions about Greenland.

"I've got it!" he said to Josephine one evening. "I'll earn the money for the new expedition by speaking about the old one."

"You mean you'll lecture across the country?"

"Yes. I don't care much for making speeches, but I will if I can raise the money we'll need."

Peary asked Matt Henson to help on the tour.

"We'll both be dressed in Eskimo furs during the hour that I talk," Peary explained. "You'll be back stage with the five Eskimo dogs that we brought back from Greenland."

"What'll I do with them?"

"When I start talking about our dogs, you'll snap your whip and march them across the stage."

"But they'll raise the roof!" said Henson. "Eskimo dogs are the noisiest ones in the world when you harness them for a march."

"The more noise they make the better," said Peary. "This will be new to Americans, a sight they'll never forget. Everyone who sees them will tell ten other people. We'll draw big crowds."

In three months he and Henson appeared before 168 audiences around the United States. Between lectures, Peary rounded up his expedition team, bought supplies, secured a ship. But time was running out. Peary needed thousands of dollars more.

"What can we do now?" asked Henson in March. "We don't have enough time to raise more money if we're to leave by April."

Peary refused to stop trying. He would find a way—and he did. He put his expedition ship, the *Falcon*, on display. For twenty-five cents a visitor could walk around her deck.

By summer Peary had raised enough money to pay for expedition supplies—food, tools, fuel.

The *Falcon* left the country in the middle of July. With Peary were Eivind Astrup, Matt Henson, and nine other men, including several scientists. There also were *two* women aboard ship, Josephine and her nurse, Susan Cross. Josephine needed nursing care for she was expecting to give birth soon.

Again Peary headed for a point far up Greenland's western coast. Instead of camping at Whale Sound, as in 1891–92, Peary pushed the ship into Bowdoin

Bay, farther to the northeast. There the expedition would be closer to the edge of the ice plateau.

"Every mile that we travel by ship will save wear and tear on ourselves and our dogs," Peary said.

The *Falcon* reached Bowdoin Bay in mid-August 1893. Peary lost no time preparing for the coming winter. He had the Eskimos, under Matt Henson, build a wooden house. Hunting parties were sent out after walrus and reindeer for their skins and meat.

"We'll soon begin dropping off supplies of food on the icecap," Peary told the men. "We'll bury our supplies every few miles along the way and mark each place with a pole."

"But we won't be heading north until next February," said Hugh Lee, a newspaper reporter. "Why haul supplies now?"

"To save time and work," Peary answered. "It's easier to move supplies in daylight before the winter night begins."

Lee began to see what Peary was driving at. The deeper they moved into the icecap now, the less work there'd be later.

Matt Henson built five new sledges. Eskimos loaded each sledge with a thousand pounds of pemmican, fresh meat, and other foods. On August 29, 1893, Peary asked Eivind Astrup to move the sledges to the icecap with a team of fifty dogs. Helping Astrup were Hugh Lee, George Carr, and James Davidson.

September 12 was a happy day for Peary and

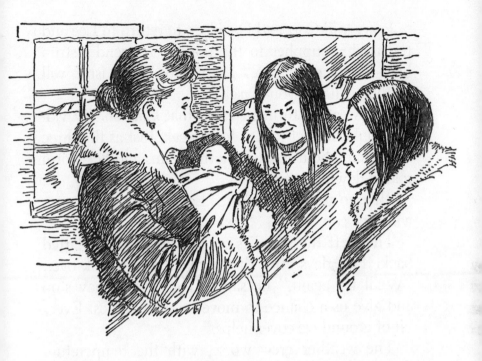

Josephine—and the entire camp. Josephine gave birth to a beautiful baby, who was named Marie Ahnighito. Eskimos came from near and far to see her, for no white child ever had been born this far north.

The very next day brought trouble.

Astrup, doubled over in pain, returned to camp with Carr and Davidson. Peary was shocked.

"What's wrong?" he asked.

"Astrup has been having sharp pains in his stomach," said Carr.

"And where is Lee?"

"With the supply sledges fifteen miles from here. We've been pinned down by bad storms."

Peary told Carr and Davidson to return to Lee and try moving supplies to the north. "I'll send Astrup back in a week or two," Peary said. "If he isn't well by then, I'll join you myself."

The weather turned so bad that Carr and Davidson could not get to Lee for a week. Just as the three men were about to push north again, another storm roared down on them.

"It's no use," said Carr. "Let's get back to camp while we can."

They left the supplies on the sledges and started back. Two days after they arrived, Peary took over. "We'll try again," he said. "The storms may stop and give us a chance to move on a few miles. Every bit of ground we cover helps."

The weather grew worse, with the temperature dropping to thirty degrees below zero. Somehow they managed to get back to the sledges. Storms whipped up to slow them. In four days they moved their supplies only fourteen miles.

"We're not getting very far," said Lee.

"Yes, but we're moving. That's better than nothing," Peary answered.

Soon after, Carr slipped while carrying a heavy box of pemmican. His back slammed down on the ice. He needed medical care at once. Peary ordered the men back to camp.

A few days later trouble struck again. All was quiet in the camp. Most of the men, including Peary, were on a hunting trip about five miles away. Josephine, her baby, and the nurse were alone in the wooden main building.

Suddenly they heard a roar. The building shook, and Josephine froze in fear on the spot. Then came the frightening noise of racing water. Josephine ran to a window. Fast-flowing water, dragging big chunks of ice, circled along the beach. A door slammed as someone charged into the house. It was Lee.

"What's happening?" Josephine asked.

"A mountain of ice just snapped off from the top of Bowdoin glacier," Lee answered. "The crash set a huge underwater wave in motion. It broke through the ice frozen over the bay—and rolled up this far."

"Has there been much damage?"

"A few of our small boats were smashed in. And we've lost most of our winter fuel. The wave tore open oil barrels as if they were made of eggshells!"

Most galling to Peary was the loss of the oil. The men would have much less fuel for their small stoves on the march across Greenland.

Blizzards struck hard during November. Soon winter's darkness, the long Arctic night, hung over the camp and seemed to freeze there. Peary gave up the idea of moving food to the ice plateau.

In December the weather improved, but it was too late and too dark to move food to the icecap. In weak moonlight the men hunted walrus and reindeer. January found Peary restless to march north.

By mid-February daylight had returned slowly. Peary was ready. But gale winds arose, holding him back several weeks.

Early in March the expedition pushed off—Peary, eight men, five Eskimo helpers, ninety-two dogs, nine fully-loaded sledges. It took the party more than a week to drag the heavy sledges thirty miles up to the icecap. Peary then sent the Eskimos back to camp.

A few days later the temperature dropped to fifty-six degrees below zero.

Soon, in the terrible cold, the men used all their remaining oil to keep warm. The only fuel left was alcohol. With it, they made small fires to melt ice for tea. Some days were so cold the ice could not be melted by the weak flame of the small alcohol stove.

In mid-March Lee came down with a badly frozen foot. Astrup took sick, sharp pains in his stomach. Neither man could go on in the cold.

"This serious crippling of my party at the very start caused me a sleepless night," Peary wrote. He brought Lee and Astrup back to camp by sledge, then quickly returned to the ice plateau.

Another giant storm arose, and gale winds whipped over the ice. A blinding blizzard stopped the advance.

"Early on Friday morning, March 23, 1894," Peary wrote, "I looked out on a scene that made me sick at heart. Half my dogs were frozen fast in the snow, some by the legs, some the tails, some by both. Two were dead. All were in a pitiable condition, their fur a mass of ice and snow—driven into it by the pitiless wind."

That day Davidson reported a pain in his heel. The expedition's doctor, Edward Vincent, examined it and hurried to Peary. "His heel is so badly frozen, I may have to cut it off," the doctor reported. Dr. Vincent and Davidson were sent back to camp with Matt Henson.

That left only Peary and three men—Entrikin, Baldwin, and Clark. They did not get very far.

For days the temperature hung between forty and sixty degrees below zero. Winds screamed for hours at a time, driving many of the dogs crazy. Every morning Peary found one or two dead dogs, frozen to the ice like queer statues. Some were smothered under wind-blown snow piles.

During one night march, Baldwin was so cold he covered his face and began breathing into his fur suit —freezing it stiff!

Baldwin could not turn his head, bend, or move. His dog team lagged behind. Peary found Baldwin, his face half frozen, barely able to breathe.

One night early in April, Clark fell asleep with his face uncovered. In the morning he was found in terrible pain—his nose frozen fast to his sleeping bag.

Peary pressed Clark's hands against his nose. "Keep them on your nose all morning," he told Clark. "The body heat of your hands will free your nose from the sleeping bag."

The next day Entrikin said his feet felt numb. They were partly frozen.

Peary and the crippled party pushed northward. By April 10, they were 128 miles from camp—but 500 long miles from Independence Bay on Greenland's northernmost shore.

The men were sick and groggy. The remaining dogs seemed half dead. There was only one thing left, Peary decided—return to camp.

"We'll take back with us only as much pemmican as we need for the return trip," Peary said. "The rest will be buried here under ice. The ice will help keep the pemmican from spoiling, and we'll be able to use it when we come this way again."

He did not say when that would be.

Then the four men turned south and headed for camp. They arrived on April 20. "Lieutenant Peary, Baldwin, Entrikin, and Clark came home from the icecap today," Lee wrote in his diary. "Entrikin's the worst. Clark's hands and feet are in bad shape and he is snow blind. Peary has the same trouble. And Baldwin is all broken down."

For the next two weeks, Dr. Vincent looked after the men. Slowly their health improved, although Davidson's heel had to be cut off.

During this time, however, Peary brooded and hardly spoke to anyone.

"This isn't like you," said Josephine. "You're never so gloomy."

"How else can I feel? My expedition has failed."

"Certainly not because of you!"

"Why not? I'm the leader."

"But you're not to blame for all that went wrong—the terrible gale winds, the freezing weather, the time lost trying to move food. You could not stop Bowdoin glacier from wrecking oil barrels. You could do nothing about the men getting sick, one after the other."

Peary shook his head. "My expedition was to reach Independence Bay and northern Greenland. We never got halfway there."

Peary knew that the *Falcon* soon would arrive from the United States with supplies. And he had nothing to report for a year's work.

Yet there was still time to make an important discovery for science—the little known meteorites!

"Meteorites? In Greenland?" Lee said, when Peary asked him along.

"They were reported in 1818 by Captain John Ross, a British explorer," Peary explained. "He told of Eskimos who used knives with iron edges. Melville Bay Eskimos said the iron came from 'iron mountains' but refused to show Ross where they were. He believed the iron supply was meteorites that hit Greenland from space centuries ago."

Lee, in good health again, agreed to go with Peary. They left camp on May 16, arriving at Melville Bay a week later. Peary brought along gifts for the bay Eskimos and made friends with them. They showed him where to find the "iron mountains." Each was a meteorite.

"They're among the biggest ones that ever landed on Earth," said Lee.

"They're a scientific find—if only we can get them to the States."

After returning to camp, Peary wrote a report on the meteorites. He would send it back with the *Falcon* to let United States scientists know of his discovery. Someday he would bring the meteorites to the United States for scientific study.

Before the *Falcon* arrived, Peary told Josephine he thought it best for her and Marie to return home.

"You both deserve far more comforts than I can give you," he said.

Peary then asked the men if they would remain with him another year.

"Will you stay, Matt?" Peary asked Henson.

"Yes—for as long as you want me, Lieutenant."

"Thank you," Peary said. "I can depend on you."

Then, one by one, the men answered, "No."

Peary was shocked. This meant they would leave Greenland on the *Falcon* in August. Peary turned to Hugh Lee, the last man to answer.

"How about you?"

"I'll stay, Lieutenant!"

"Do you mean it? Do you really mean it?"

"Sure I do," said Lee.

"Wonderful! Wonderful!" Peary cried out in joy.

Now his hopes soared again. Matt Henson and Hugh Lee would bring a good run of luck. Peary again would stand on Greenland's northernmost shore and look out across the Arctic Ocean.

CHAPTER SIX

A MAGNIFICENT FLAG

April 1, 1895 . . .

After a busy winter of hunting, Peary, Henson, and Lee left the base camp at Bowdoin Bay for the ice plateau. Each man drove his own dog team.

Six Eskimos helped move the heavily loaded sledges out of the base camp. In four days the party marched north 125 miles. Peary was now at the same area where he had buried 1,400 pounds of pemmican in the spring of 1894. The men stopped to search for this much-needed cache of food.

This was Peary's plan:

Step One. Find the pemmican cache. Let the tired dogs rest for a day or two. Feed them well on fresh walrus meat. Peary's Reason: "The pemmican cache is 125 miles inland—an advance base for us. If we rest the dogs here, they'll be starting off fresh again, 125 miles *nearer* to Independence Bay and Greenland's northern coast."

Step Two. Take off most of our walrus and reindeer meat and bury it in the ice. Peary's Rea-

SON: "We'll be putting away a reserve supply of fresh food for our return trip. Then the last 125 miles back to Bowdoin Bay, from here, will be easy."

STEP THREE. Load the pemmican on the sledges, in place of the walrus and reindeer meat. PEARY'S REASON: "The pemmican will serve as an ace in the hole—if we find nothing else to eat. And it's lighter than our walrus and reindeer supply. That means our dogs won't have to work as hard getting us to Independence Bay."

For twenty-four hours Peary and the men searched for the 1,400 pounds of pemmican. They crisscrossed over five miles of ice and snow looking for it.

They found no trace of the food supply.

Should they continue—without the pemmican?

Peary had to make up his mind fast. Yes, he would take a chance! But what about Henson and Lee?

"We'll turn back if either of you don't care to go on without the pemmican," Peary told them.

"I'll go," said Henson.

"Count me in," added Lee.

Peary slapped them on the back. "That's fine! With luck, we'll find musk oxen to make up for the lost pemmican. The Eskimos will go back, before storms strand them here."

On April 17 Peary, Henson, and Lee started out for Independence Bay with forty-two dogs.

Lee soon came down sick with a bad cold, headaches, and frostbitten toes. Peary ordered him "to bed" on the supply sledge. Without Lee's help, Peary and Henson had an even harder time feeding walrus meat to the hungry dogs.

At feeding time, wrote Peary, "howling dogs swept across the ice and fell upon the meat. . . . Here before us were forty-two savage, powerful dogs, mad with the struggle for food."

A savage blizzard delayed them forty-eight hours. Two dogs died in the storm and were fed to the others to save food. The dogs grew weak. They averaged two miles an hour on a march. When Peary tried to speed them up, they panted for breath.

"They're getting weaker," he said to Henson. "I'm afraid more dogs will die. If they do, we'll feed them to the others—until we find fresh meat."

"That better be soon," said Henson.

Near the end of April they reached their highest altitude on the icecap—7,865 feet above sea level. They had covered 400 miles. But the Arctic Ocean lay 200 miles to the north.

The icecap sloped downward, easing their marches. Yet every morning Peary and Henson found one or two dogs dead of hunger. By May 1 only seventeen dogs were still alive.

"They've eaten the last of the walrus meat," Henson reported.

"Some of the dogs are so weak, they'll soon die," Peary said. "There's nothing we can do for them. Kill the weakest dog, and feed it to the others.

Henson, fond of his huskies, was not willing at first. But their lives depended on reaching the northern coast, where musk oxen grazed. At the end of each day, Henson killed the weakest dog and fed it to the remaining huskies. On they crept. In a week, there were just eleven dogs left.

On May 6 they sighted Independence Bay.

"Never shall I forget that time and scene," wrote Peary, "three weary men and nine starved dogs, standing there in the frozen desert."

They dragged themselves forward and reached the frozen waters of the ice-jammed Arctic Ocean. Somewhere to the endless white north lay a route to the North Pole. But Peary had no desire to dwell over it now.

FOOD!

That was his only thought.

Peary and Henson set up a tent for Lee, now very weak. While Lee rested, Peary and Henson searched for food. A few miles from the tent, Peary believed his eyes were playing tricks on him. Off to the side a white rock seemed to be jumping. It was a hare.

"Get it, Matt!" Peary shouted to Henson, nearest the animal.

Henson fired and missed. He fired again and missed again. The hare scampered off. Henson had time for one more shot. This time he hit.

The fresh meat, their first in weeks, gave Peary and

Henson strength. They hiked several more miles to a valley where Peary found musk ox tracks. Up ahead were musk oxen.

Peary and Henson moved slowly toward the herd. They were forty yards away when the leader, a huge bull, heard them. The bull turned angrily. The other musk oxen wheeled around toward Peary. They lowered their heads, pointing their horns at him.

Peary thought the surprised animals might charge. Rather than wait, he rushed at them. As he ran, he fired at the lead bull. It sank to the ground. The herd fell back. Now Henson's rifle crackled fire, and another musk ox dropped. They killed four more—and then feasted.

"What animals hunger makes of men!" Peary noted. "Never have I tasted more delicious food than was that tender, raw, warm meat—a mouthful here and a mouthful there, cut from the animal as I skinned it."

Peary and Henson returned to Lee, who gained strength after eating musk ox steaks. During the next few days, as the weather cleared, Peary examined and made careful notes at Independence Bay. He saw much more of Greenland's northern coast and of the the Arctic Ocean than he had in 1892.

Soon after, the men loaded their sledges with musk ox meat. Then with their nine well-fed and well-rested dogs they started home.

But the bitter cold 600-mile return trip brought on

more suffering. Icy storms slashed at them. The musk ox supply did not last very long because of the long delays. One by one, the dogs died or were killed for food. With 300 miles to go, Lee fainted.

Peary turned back for him.

"I'm finished," Lee said.

Peary lifted Lee and carried him to a sledge.

"Don't bother with me," Lee muttered. "You're risking your lives. Go on without me. Save yourselves! Good-by . . . Good luck."

Peary put his arm around Lee.

"We will have no more of that kind of talk. We will all get home, or none of us will."

Straining every inch of the way they averaged twenty miles a day over the next two weeks. On June 24 Bowdoin Bay came into view. Wrote Peary:

"We had besides a little tea and milk, four biscuits remaining for our supper and breakfast. One dog was still alive. To him I fed a pair of sealskin boots and a few yards of rawhide line."

The men—and the last dog—stumbled into camp half-dead. For a week they did nothing but sleep and eat, eat and sleep. As the days wore on, Peary became bitter over having failed again. He refused to credit himself for a most amazing journey of 1,200 miles. He felt ashamed of leading an expedition that had suffered so greatly.

In August 1895, the supply ship *Kite* arrived at

Bowdoin Bay. She was to bring Peary, Henson, and Lee home.

First the *Kite* stopped at Melville Bay, where Peary had found three meteorites in 1894. The two "smaller" meteorites were loaded on the ship. One weighed 5,500 pounds, the other 1,000 pounds. They were to be given to the American Museum of Natural History in New York City.

"The third meteorite is much too large and too heavy for this ship," Peary told Lee. "I'll come back for it soon in a larger ship."

Soon turned out to be the very next summer. Peary returned to Greenland with Matt Henson and Hugh Lee in July 1896.

Peary brought along powerful machinery to lift the 36-ton meteorite out of "its frozen bed of centuries." This was back-breaking work that kept a dozen men in sweat. While tugging at the monster meteorite with chains, the work crew sang:

> *"Oh my Johnny Voker*
> *We will turn this heavy joker*
> *We will roll and rock it over*
> *We will turn the heavy joker*
> *Oh my Johnny Voker—HAUL!"*

The men "turned the heavy joker" out of the ice and moved it to the edge of the shore at Melville Bay. They worked slowly, sliding the chain-pulled meteorite over steel rails resting on heavy wooden planks. Soon the waters froze and began to clog with ice. The ship was in danger of being crushed.

Peary had to leave the meteorite at the water's edge and go home.

In the summer of 1897 he returned—with Josephine and Marie, now nearly four years old. The ship anchored near the meteorite. Peary's work crew built a small "railway" bridge from the shore to the ship. On the rails the men put together a railway car to carry the meteorite across the water.

On the day it was to be moved to the ship, Peary held a ceremony. He draped an American flag over the meteorite. Then he had Josphine pull one lever of the machine that was to lift the huge prize. As it began to rise, Peary handed a small bottle of wine to Marie.

"Say 'I name thee Ahnighito,'" Peary said to his daughter, "and throw the bottle against the rock."

"I name thee Ahnighito," said Marie Ahnighito, and the men cheered.

Peary brought the meteorite home and turned it over to the American Museum of Natural History. Scientists were amazed to see this huge mass of iron and nickel from outer space.

A few months later Peary was invited to England by the Royal Geographical Society of London. He received a gold medal for his "unequalled journeys across Greenland's ice."

While in London, Peary told of his newest plan to reach the Pole.

"I'll try to get beyond Greenland's northern coast —by ship," he explained. "I'll set up a base camp there. Then, by dog team, I'll make a 400-mile dash for the Pole over the frozen Arctic Ocean."

"Why do you want so much to reach the North Pole?" asked a British reporter.

"Because it *is* the Pole. Reaching it will test man's mind, test man's courage, test man's strength. That means he can reach the Pole."

A British newspaper publisher heard of Peary's Arctic adventures and polar plans. He offered one of his ships, the *Windward*, as a gift to Peary. The *Windward* had once been a British polar ship.

The gift pleased Peary. He could leave for the Arctic next summer! Peary immediately returned to the United States to prepare for the expedition. He requested a five-year leave of absence from the Navy—and got it.

"I should be able to start out in a few months," he said to Josephine in the spring of 1898.

"Who will go with you?" she asked.

"Matt Henson only. Hugh Lee is not strong enough. Besides, the smaller the expedition, the better our chances. I'm sure that with Matt Henson and several Eskimos I'll have all the help I need."

Josephine dreaded asking the next question.

"How long will you be gone?"

At first Peary did not answer.

"Please tell me now, Bert. What are your plans?"

"We may not reach the Pole during the first year," Peary began. "If not, we'll try again a second year—and if need be, a third, and a fourth."

"You mean this could be a four-year expedition?"

"Yes, but I'll do my best to see it's not!"

After that, Josephine said little about the expedition. Peary began to fret over her silence. Was she unhappy over his four-year plan? Sometimes she would remain in her room for hours.

Then one evening, in the summer of 1898, Josephine seemed happy. Her good cheer pleased Peary.

"It's fine to see you this way again," he said.

"I've a surprise for you!" broke in Josephine. "I've finished it!"

"What are you talking about?"

"Close your eyes—and don't dare open them until I tell you."

Peary did as he was told, then sat back and waited. The minutes ticked by. He heard Josephine moving in the room, climbing a chair, tapping on the wall. He could make out a familiar rustling sound but couldn't quite place it.

"Open your eyes," said Josephine.

Peary opened his eyes. Hanging from the living room wall was the most beautiful American flag he had ever seen. It was pure silk.

"I made it for you," Josephine said. "May it bring you good luck and the one goal you seek."

Peary touched the hand-sewn flag. He was deeply moved.

"It's magnificent," he said. "How wonderful of you, my dear. This flag will never leave my side."

CHAPTER SEVEN

"MY DREAM IS ENDED"

JUST west of northern Greenland lies Canada's icy Ellesmere Island. Two narrow channels of water separate northern Greenland and Ellesmere Island. One is Kennedy Channel, the other Robeson Channel.

Peary hoped, in 1898, to force his ship, the *Windward*, through BOTH waterways to the Arctic Ocean. This would put him at the northern edge of Ellesmere Island. He and Henson would save hundreds of miles of tough marches over trackless ice fields.

They would be fresh and strong for the 400-mile dash to the Pole.

"But why are we going to Ellesmere Island?" Henson asked. "Why not push off for the Pole from Greenland?"

"Very little is known about Ellesmere Island. I want to see for myself what it's like," answered Peary. "It lured one of America's greatest Arctic explorers— someone I greatly admired as a boy."

"Who was that?" asked Henson.

"Elisha Kent Kane," said Peary. "In the 1850s he

explored the Arctic region now named after him—
Kane Basin. Another American who explored Ellesmere Island is Adolphus Washington Greely. In 1881
he set up a base camp for scientists at Fort Conger.
They were only about 500 miles from the Pole."

"How long did they stay?"

"About three years. Then they ran into trouble.
Their supply ship from the States couldn't break
through the ice in Kennedy Channel. Greely and his
twenty-four men left Fort Conger and headed south
toward the ship. Only Greely and six men got back
alive."

"And the others?"

"They starved to death."

All went well with Peary and Henson at the start
of the trip. They stopped at Etah, Greenland, for a
short visit in July 1898.

Peary traded with the Eskimos for dogs, fresh reindeer and walrus meat, fur skins. The dogs and the
supplies were loaded on the *Windward*. Peary also
found Eskimos who joined the expedition. They were
crack hunters, sledge builders, dog drivers.

From Etah, the *Windward* turned north and entered Kane Basin in mid-August. Freezing weather
suddenly set in. Ice began to form around the ship
as she nosed toward Kennedy Channel.

On August 18 the *Windward* inched through an
opening in the ice. She moved ahead slowly—then
was blocked by a blanket of floating ice.

The *Windward* slipped toward the shore. She managed to reach Cape D'Urville on Ellesmere Island. The temperature dipped to thirteen degrees below zero. Steel-strong ice trapped the ship.

She was locked in Kane Basin for the winter.

This was a serious setback for Peary. It put an end to his hope of reaching Ellesmere Island's northern coast by ship. He now had to change his plans—or admit defeat.

Peary was never one to give up easily. He might still be able to reach the Pole:

IF he used Cape D'Urville as a base camp.

IF he took off supplies from the ship and began hunting for more fresh meat.

IF he set up camp closer to the Pole.

IF he stored food at this advance camp.

Peary carefully studied his maps of Ellesmere Island. Where was the best site for an advance camp?

"Here it is!" he called to Henson one evening. "Fort Conger!"

"Greely's old camp?"

"Why not? The wooden building Greely used may still be standing."

"How far is Fort Conger from Cape D'Urville?" Henson asked.

"About 250 miles," Peary answered. "We should be able to move our supplies there on sledges. With Fort Conger as our advance camp, we'll have a good chance of reaching the North Pole next spring."

They set to work at once.

First, with Eskimo hunters helping, they spent weeks searching for fresh meat. They found bears, musk oxen, wild hares, walrus. Then they began to move supplies northward to Fort Conger by sledges and dog teams. Peary's idea was to bury supplies in the ice at points about twenty miles apart.

The men traveled and worked slowly, for the darkness of the Arctic night was upon them. In November moonlight appeared for only a few hours during any 24-hour period. By December the caches of food were buried along a 125-mile route to Fort Conger.

On December 28, 1898, Peary wrote:

"In spite of delays I felt well satisfied with the work. I had my supplies half way to Fort Conger. . . ."

The next day Peary, Henson, and two Eskimos started out for Fort Conger from the last cache. They sped along frozen Kennedy Channel on light sledges. Peary hoped to arrive at the fort in five days.

"We'll see what condition it's in—then we'll start hauling supplies to the fort," he said to Henson.

Suddenly the weather took a turn for the worse. The temperature dropped sharply . . . 40 . . . 45 . . . 50 . . . 60 degrees below zero. Biting winds snapped at the men and dogs and set their teeth to chattering. The icy gales took their breath away.

Numb with cold, they plunged through gloomy darkness. Ice and sky seemed frozen into one black desert. Around them were stretches of sharp-jutting ice. It had been pushed up from Kennedy Channel by the great pressure of expanding ice. Blocked by the Ellesmere and Greenland shore lines, the ice piled up high at many places in the channel.

Across this rough ice, sometimes towering more than 100 feet, pushed the men and dogs. But their advance was slow. Food began to run out.

"Just south of Cape Defosse we ate the last of our biscuit, just north of it the last of our beans," wrote Peary. And soon after, "a dog was killed for food."

On January 6, 1899, the half-starved, half-frozen men stumbled into broken-down Fort Conger. Scattered around the wooden cabin were a few remains of the Greely expedition—tables, chairs, cots, books, papers, cups and saucers, a stove.

Henson quickly lighted a fire in the stove. As Peary warmed himself by the fire, he winced several times.

"Anything wrong, Lieutenant?" asked Henson.

"I've a pain in my right foot," answered Peary. "It feels numb—almost wooden."

"Can you move your toes?"

"I don't think so."

Henson took off Peary's sealskin boots and rabbit-skin shoes. Both of Peary's feet were badly frozen. The toes were black and blue. It might be a long time before Peary could walk again.

Henson rubbed Peary's toes, then helped him to a cot. Peary loosened his clothing to make himself

comfortable. For the moment, Henson thought his eyes were failing him. Wrapped around Peary's waist was an American flag!

"My wife made it," Peary said to the surprised Henson. "I've promised to keep it with me always."

Worn out, Peary fell asleep. The next morning he awoke to a sharp throbbing in both feet. Peary could hardly take a step. He fell back on his cot.

The throbbing pains grew worse. The days stretched into weeks while Peary fretted. Was this the end of his dream to reach the North Pole?

The question distressed him. Every day he tested his feet to see if he could stand. The pain grew worse, but his fighting spirit lashed him.

One morning a wild Arctic wind whipped across the ice field. The wind shook the weak and old cabin, half buried in snowdrifts. Peary, alone, rose from his cot. His face twisted in pain, he managed to stand on his swollen feet. Then he sat down and wrote on the wall nearest the cot:

Inveniam viam aut faciam. This was Latin for: "I shall find a way or make one."

Henson and the two Eskimos soon returned to the cabin from a hunt for musk oxen.

"We're leaving," Peary said. "We're going back to the *Windward* so that the ship doctor can take care of my feet."

"But you can't stand," protested Henson.

"I've had my fill of doing nothing. I can make it

back by sledge. Just strap me down so that I don't bounce too much."

Peary left Fort Conger on February 18. Henson carried him out to a sledge and tied him to it.

The 250-mile return trip took eleven days. For Peary, never free from stabs of pain on the jolting sled, the going was rough. Furious winds roared down on the men, blinding them with driving snow. They crawled along, hardly able to see a yard ahead. With the temperature at sixty-five degrees below zero, they reached the *Windward.*

The ship doctor examined Peary's frozen feet. His toes were "raw stumps with open sores"—and bare bones.

"I'm afraid I'll have to cut off eight toes," said the doctor.

"Just leave enough for me to stand on when I get to the Pole," muttered Peary.

The doctor removed eight of Peary's toes, leaving only the little toe on each foot.

"You had better go back with the *Windward* when she returns home," said the doctor. "You need medical care and rest."

"I do not intend to leave," said Peary. "When this four-year expedition ends, or when I have reached the Pole, I will return—but not until then."

"Be reasonable! You're not in the best of health, you know."

"I have no reason to make a fuss. I will stay."

Peary could walk only with crutches. Yet a month later, he set out again for Fort Conger. Henson tied him to a supply sledge for the 250-mile trip. With Eskimos helping, they made a series of supply trips between Fort Conger and Cape D'Urville. Tons of food were moved to the fort.

"This will be our advance base again next winter for a march on the Pole," Peary told Henson.

In the meantime Peary decided to explore Ellesmere Island west of Kane Basin.

Peary changed his plans in March 1900.

Instead of trying for the Pole, he chose to head for Greenland's northern coast. It was about a day's travel by sledge.

"Why this change?" asked Henson.

"The dogs are not up to it," Peary said. "They don't have the strength to pull our supplies to the Pole. But we can explore Greenland if we travel lightly. We'll hunt musk oxen for food."

"What about the Pole?"

"We'll try again next year—and the year after if we have to."

On April 11 Peary and Henson left Fort Conger. They crossed frozen Robeson Channel, then moved eastward along Greenland's northern coast. In below zero weather they pushed on until they had covered more than 350 miles—the entire northern coast.

In May, Peary's observations showed that he was now standing at the "most northern" point in Greenland. He named the area Cape Morris Jesup, after one of the men who had helped him raise money.

Peary wrote a short report of his trip to Cape Morris Jesup. Then he snipped two small pieces from Josephine's American flag. He buried them, along with the report, under a pile of stones.

"This is how I'll mark every important place I reach in the Arctic, with a piece of my wife's flag," Peary told Henson. "And someday I'll do the same at the North Pole."

Peary hoped to reach the Pole during the coming winter, 1900–01, or at the latest, during the winter of 1901–02.

He had no luck either time.

In the winter of 1900–01 Peary, Henson, and one Eskimo shivered at Fort Conger preparing for a dash to the Pole. They started toward it on April 5, 1901, but the cold weather was too much for them.

Peary headed for Cape Sabine, to the south. A ship was due there from the United States. Peary reached the ship on May 6, his birthday, and found a birthday surprise—Josephine and Marie Ahnighito!

"Why have you both come so far?" Peary asked, with great pleasure.

"I've worried about you, ever since the dreadful winter of 1899," answered Josephine. "We heard you couldn't stand after your toes were amputated."

"I'm fine—now that I have both of you again."

Peary refused to talk about himself. Josephine was

shocked at the way he looked. Deep wrinkles lined his thin face. His cheekbones pressed against dark bags under his eyes. His shoulders stooped, as if he were still bucking icy winds.

"When can we have you with us for good?" asked Josephine.

"After I reach the Pole—and nail the most beautiful flag in the world to it," answered Peary.

In the winter of 1901–02 Peary was determined. This might be his last chance to succeed in his goal to reach the North Pole.

For months he and Henson worked hard getting their sledges and supplies in order. In February 1902, they advanced northward beyond Fort Conger. On April 6 they stood at the very edge of Ellesmere Island's northern coast. Stinging winds blasted at them in temperatures as low as fifty-seven below zero.

Peary, Henson, two Eskimos, and the weary dogs pushed across the ice-covered Arctic Ocean. Would the ice hold? Peary was ever mindful that it might crack under their sledges and rip wide open.

Soon the ice began to churn and grind and spread.

"Through this ice we struggled," wrote Peary. "The dogs floundered almost uselessly—occasionally disappearing for a moment. . . . We were obliged to wait for floating pieces to crush close enough together to let us pass from one to the other."

Peary's observations showed that he had reached a latitude of 84 degrees 17 minutes on April 21, 1902.

This was the farthest north any man had reached in the Western Hemisphere.

Peary was 375 miles from the North Pole but could not advance another step. He had been stopped once again. Peary turned his back on the Pole and headed for Ellesmere Island.

With the saddest feeling he had known, he wrote:

"The game is off. My dream of sixteen years is ended. . . . I have made the best fight I knew. I believe it has been a good one. But I cannot accomplish the impossible."

CHAPTER EIGHT

THE FLAG GOES FORWARD

PEARY had lost hope of ever reaching the North Pole. Yet this feeling did not last long. Within a few days, he began toying with a new idea.

It was this:

"A polar ship! A ship that can smash through Arctic ice—even in the dead of winter."

Henson agreed. "She'd put up at the top of Ellesmere Island faster than sledges. We'd reach the Pole before the ice started breaking up."

"The ship I have in mind," said Peary, "would have an engine as powerful as a battleship's. She'd also have masts and sails. She'd be able to save her fuel in strong winds—or keep moving if falling ice snapped off her propeller."

"That's a great ship, Lieutenant. Only trouble is—she's never been built. Where would you get her?"

"I'll have to build her myself!"

That was a tall order, as Peary was to learn.

He received a cold welcome on his return to the United States in 1902. He was brushed off as a man who had failed.

"Peary? What's he done?" asked those who judged him harshly. "Four years in the Arctic—FOUR more years—and he still hasn't reached the North Pole."

They did not understand that the Pole wasn't Peary's for the asking. They did not know it as he did —a guarded, shadow of a prize. They did not care that he was coming closer and closer.

With each passing year, Peary had learned something new about Arctic travel: ice forms, currents, tides, sledges, dogs, storms, glaciers, geography, Eskimos, animal life, hunting, supplies, equipment.

Peary had no money in 1902. Nor was there much chance of his raising any to build the dream ship.

He had best get back to work.

In the fall, Peary reported for Navy duty at Washington, D.C. He found Navy men avoiding him as a "crazy weather-beaten fool." Hardly anyone bothered to speak to him during the day.

"I felt," wrote Peary, "as if I had wandered back like a lost cat!"

Peary buckled down to work. Soon the Navy promoted him to the rank of Commander.

Meanwhile, in his spare time, he designed a 600-ton polar ship. She was to be 184 feet long and 35 feet wide. One evening in the spring of 1903 he showed drawings of the ship to Josephine.

She would have 1,000-horsepower engines, explained Peary, enough to move three or four ships her size. She'd have a sharp, chisel-like bow of iron to split open ice. Her propeller would be easy to repair if damaged by ice.

"We'll be able to pull up her rudder on deck in ice-packed waters," Peary said. "And she'll have a smooth, rounded bottom to lift her."

"Lift her?" asked Josephine.

"That's right. Ice won't be able to grip her curved sides and crush them. As the ice closes in, she'll lift right up out of it—almost the way a pit squirts out of a squeezed orange! And her weight will smash ice."

Peary now needed money to build the ship.

For help, the determined explorer turned to the Peary Arctic Club. This was a small group of businessmen who backed him. They had raised the money for his 1898–1902 expeditions. The club got behind Peary again. Then more good news followed. On August 29, 1903, Josephine gave birth to a son. He was named Robert Edwin Peary, Jr.

By July, the Peary Arctic Club raised enough money to build the polar ship. Her keel was laid October 15, 1904.

On March 23, 1905, the ship was lowered into the water. She was named the *Roosevelt*, in honor of President Theodore Roosevelt.

Early in July, Peary was ready to start out on his seventh trip to the Arctic.

"This time I'll reach the Pole," he said to Josephine. "The *Roosevelt* is a fine ship. And she has a great skipper."

"Who is he?" asked Josephine.

"Captain Robert A. Bartlett."

"Bartlett? I know that name. Wasn't he with you before?"

"Yes," answered Peary. "He served as a mate aboard the *Windward* in 1898 and 1899. Bartlett is a master seaman."

The *Roosevelt* left the United States in mid-July 1905, and sailed north.

Peary spent much of each day on a small rope ladder high in the rigging of a swaying mast. Just above him in the crow's nest stood Captain Bartlett. Both men watched the ice closely, looking for openings in the frozen waters. Peary called his findings up to Bartlett. Then, in a lusty voice, Bartlett shouted his commands to the wheelsman.

Bartlett pushed the ship on:

"Give it to 'em, Teddy, give it to 'em! Harder! That's the way!"

The ship's mighty zigzag blows opened lanes of water in the ice.

"Give it to 'em, Teddy! Keep moving! Keep moving!" cried Bartlett.

For days the ship crunched deeper into the Arctic.

"In all my experience," wrote Peary, "I recall nothing more exciting than the thrill, the crash, the shock of hurtling the *Roosevelt* at the ice. . . . Again I see Bartlett in the crow's nest, jumping up and down like a madman, swearing, shouting to the ship. . . ."

The *Roosevelt* won her first major battle against Arctic ice on September 5, 1905. On that day, she sailed into Cape Sheridan at the northeastern corner of Ellesmere Island.

Peary now was 350 miles nearer the Pole than in 1898, when ice trapped the *Windward* at Cape D'Urville. The *Roosevelt* had saved Peary and the men and dogs weeks of hard sledging over ice.

About 400 miles to the north lay the North Pole.

The expedition's first job was to take supplies from the *Roosevelt*—soon gripped in endless ice. Huts and igloos were built for the Eskimos and crew.

Peary then sent out hunting parties to add to the food supply.

All through the long dark winter Cape Sheridan was a busy base. By mid-February 1906, Peary had worked out a "relay" system for his dash to the Pole.

"We'll start out in two groups—a pioneer party and the main party," Peary said to Henson. "You'll lead the pioneer party. You will break trail for my main party. It will be divided into five groups."

"How far ahead of you will I be with my men?" Henson asked.

"Two or three days. Every fifty miles or so I'll send one of the sections back to bring up supplies for us. But I won't return for supplies. I'll join with you for the final dash to the Pole."

Would this relay system work?

The answer, Peary knew, depended on the ice and

MATT HENSON

how firmly it remained frozen. Strong winds and changing tides might move the ice too fast. As it swayed, the ice could split open and form wide lanes of water. Those far to the north would be stranded. They might never return to land.

On March 2 the expedition headed north, with Henson paving the way.

"I get so impatient, I do not want to stop—but keep right on and on," Peary noted.

The advance bogged down on March 26, 1906. The moving ice had opened a lead of water that stopped Henson and his Eskimos. Peary overtook him in a few days. For six days, the men camped at the edge of the two-mile wide lead waiting for it to freeze over. Soon a thin sheet of ice began to form on the water. By April 2 the ice was strong enough to support the men, dogs, and sledges.

More delays followed as gale-blown ice floes crashed into each other and pushed up walls of ice thirty feet high.

By mid-April food was low. Peary decided to keep pushing north with Henson and his Eskimos.

"I'm sending two Eskimos back toward the base camp," he said to Henson. "We've got to know what the ice is like behind us. If it's breaking up we must return—or we may never get back."

"Let them get started right now," Henson said.

In less than twenty-four hours the Eskimos were back. They reported having been stopped by wide leads of open water to the *south*. Peary, Henson, and the Eskimos were in for trouble.

They had been cut off from land.

"Let's make a dash for the Pole from here," Peary said to Henson. "We have enough pemmican to last for two weeks or so."

"What about food for the dogs?"

"We'll kill those that are too weak to go on and feed them to the others."

The five Eskimos agreed to go along. For nearly a week the party marched on the Pole. Soon the men were frostbitten, sick, weak.

On April 21, 1906, Peary figured his exact position with a reading from the sun. He had reached 87 degrees 6 minutes north latitude. This was the farthest north any man ever had reached. And this was as far as Peary could go. He was 174 miles from the Pole.

Peary decided to turn south for camp after looking "at the drawn faces of my comrades, at the skeleton figures of my few dogs, at my nearly empty sledges. . . ."

Before heading back, Peary had one job left. He opened his fur suit and pulled out a piece of the American flag wrapped around his waist. Carefully he cut off a small piece of the flag. He sealed this snipped-out piece in a bottle and buried it in the ice.

The men started south on April 22. The movement of the ice worried Henson.

"The ice is moving fast," he said. "Where will it take us?"

"If we head south we should reach the coast. If we keep drifting eastward too fast, we'll end up somewhere in the Atlantic!"

There was no time to lose. Peary had to push south and touch down somewhere on Greenland. The ice floes were carrying the men out to the high seas.

This was a race for life.

A few days after they began the return march, a blizzard lashed at the men. They stumbled forward against cruel winds that all but ripped them apart. Almost every day a dog died and was used as food. Sledges were broken up for firewood.

They were now 200 miles from Greenland and food. Peary felt sure they would reach the coast if only they kept moving south. Early in May, they were stopped in their tracks.

Ahead lay open water *at least two miles across*.

They were cut off again.

For five days they could do little but stare at the water and hope it would freeze over. On the fifth day a thin sheet of ice began to form on the surface.

Could this newly formed ice hold their weight?

Peary had to decide his next move quickly. *"Wait for the ice to freeze tight?"* The lead might widen while he waited. Unable to advance, they would drift eastward to sea. *"Try crossing on thin ice!"* The ice might snap under their weight. All would drown.

Peary gave the order to head for Greenland.

"We must take the chance," he said, "or none of us will get back."

The men were warned not to step down on the ice—but to "slide" across it.

"Keep your legs wide apart and move fast, so that you're not standing on any one spot too long. If a man falls through the ice, there will be no chance to save him. Good luck to each of you."

The lightest Eskimo started across. The ice dipped but did not crack. The handful of dogs, harnessed to the last remaining sledge, followed about fifty feet behind. Then came Peary, Henson, and the four other Eskimos spaced about fifty feet apart.

The ice swayed and curved under their weight. One wrong step would split it wildly like broken glass. Suddenly Peary heard a nervous scream.

"God help him! . . . Which one is it?" Peary said, half aloud. He listened for splashing sounds and more screams. All he heard was the scrape of his snow-shoes across the ice. The last Eskimo, thinking he would fall, had screamed—but did not stumble or go down.

The long-suffering column slipped across the ice. After what seemed hours, the lead Eskimo reached across to the other "shore" of ice. Minutes later, the dogs scampered onto it. Then came Peary . . . Henson . . . the Eskimos, one by one.

Just as the last man reached safety, the sheet of ice split and parted. The lead widened again. The expedition had cheated death by a matter of seconds.

Yet Peary was bitter. He had again been thrown back by the Arctic shield around the Pole. "The story of my life has been told," he wrote, "and the word *failure* is stamped across it."

CHAPTER NINE

ONE FIGHT MORE

FOR a week the party pressed forward in below zero weather. The men were so weak with hunger they could hardly talk. Only four dogs remained alive.

Early in May 1906, Peary sighted the snow-covered mountains of Greenland's northern coast. By now the men were almost dead from starving. They killed the weakest dog and ate it raw. On May 12 they reached land.

"We've got to find fresh food today," Peary muttered to Henson.

Peary told the men to rest on a rocky hill. He climbed to the top, then headed inland. As he walked along, he loaded his rifle. During the next hour, Peary's rifle fire could be heard along the coast.

About ten minutes after the last shot, Peary returned carrying four plump hares.

The next day they headed west toward Ellesmere Island and the *Roosevelt*. Carefully they searched for musk ox tracks. Suddenly Peary came upon a fresh trail. It seemed to have been made by men swaying behind a sledge.

"We've got to find them," Peary said. "They are in trouble—and they're traveling *away* from the ship."

Two Eskimos were sent eastward in search of the lost party. Then Peary, Henson, and the other three Eskimos spread out to hunt for game.

In the morning the two Eskimos returned. With them were four men who had lost their way after leaving Peary in March. One of the starving men, numb with cold, carried a "bow" with which he hoped to hunt hares. The bow was a strand of leather tied around both ends of a long spoon! The "arrow" was a sliver of wood from a snowshoe.

"They were exhausted," wrote Peary. "They had lived for a few days by chewing their spare skin boots. They came back skull-faced. . . ."

Now there were eleven men to feed. Peary knew they could lose no time in finding food. Two days later, they ate the last of their hares.

They were nowhere near the *Roosevelt*. Nor were there any signs of animal tracks in sight.

One evening, just after they killed a dog for supper and were dividing it, the men heard an Eskimo shout!

"Oomingmuksue! Oomingmuksue!"

That was Eskimo for musk oxen. Seven had been spotted about six miles away. Seven musk oxen! Here was enough food for the party.

Grabbing his rifle and bullets, Peary raced to the

animals. Every mile or so he stopped to catch his breath, then sped on.

Peary rushed at the musk oxen like a wild man. All seven were shot down. Peary and his men had enough food to get back to the *Roosevelt.*

Soon after, they reached the western corner of Greenland and crossed frozen Robeson Channel. Another march put them on Ellesmere Island and Cape Sheridan. The *Roosevelt* sat locked in ice just as they had left her.

Every muscle in Peary's body ached. His sore feet and legs were badly puffed. The lashing icy winds left his eyes bloodshot and misty, his skin wrinkled and cracked.

Peary had bowed to the Pole again. And this latest Arctic push seemed so small on the map.

"To think that I have failed once more, that I shall never have a chance to win again," he wrote.

On June 2, 1906, only one week after his return, Peary surprised every one aboard the ship.

"I am leaving on another expedition," he announced. "The ship will not be free for another month or two. That gives me plenty of time to explore along Ellesmere's northern coast."

"But, Commander, your feet," protested Henson. "They're puffed to twice their regular size—worse than mine. You can hardly stand."

"A little exercise will do me good," smiled Peary.

"I don't expect you to come along, Matt. You've done more than your share for me."

Peary found three Eskimos willing to go with him. He had two goals on this 600-mile sledging trip:

The first: to reach Cape Columbia. This was Ellesmere's most northern area, the most northern point of land in the Western Hemisphere.

The second: to explore the "farthest-west" point on Ellesmere's northern coast. No one knew for sure how far west it really was.

Peary and the Eskimos reached Cape Columbia on June 6. In two hours they climbed 1,800 feet to the top of a steep mountain. Peary cut off a small piece of Josephine's flag and put it in a tin can. He buried the can along with a brief report of his "farthest-north" effort to reach the Pole.

On June 28 he reached his "farthest-west." With food running low, he could go no farther. Again he climbed to the top of a peak, some 1,600 feet high, and buried the fifth piece of Josephine's flag. Peary named the area Cape Thomas Hubbard (now called Cape Stallworthy) after one of his backers.

Then he headed for the *Roosevelt*, more than 300 miles to the east. They dragged their sledge over slushy, ankle-deep waters. Soon the men reached an area where the water was too deep. They were stopped—until Peary came up with a plan:

He knew that each Eskimo had several sealskin "balloons." These were waterproof bags used during a seal hunt. During a hunt, an Eskimo blew air into the bags and tied their ends, just as a child does with rubber balloons. After an Eskimo harpooned a seal, he fastened the balloons to the dead animal. The balloons kept it afloat. The seal could be moved long distances in the water with no great strain.

Peary asked each Eskimo to blow up his sealskin balloons and tie them to the sledge. It floated easily! But the men had to wade across, sometimes up to their armpits in ice-cold waters. The dogs swam beside them, gasping for breath to keep afloat.

Peary's feet—aching with hot pain "up to the knees"—were in terrible shape. His boots were worn through at the bottoms and were of little use. Peary covered the holes with flattened-out pieces of tin from empty pemmican cans.

"Can you imagine a man with his toes gone doing this? Peary did it!" So wrote Captain Bartlett on July 26, when the party reached the *Roosevelt*.

Yet the very next day Peary surprised Captain Bartlett even more! The captain had come to report bad news to him:

During the first spring thaw the *Roosevelt* was badly damaged by bobbing chunks of ice. Her stern post, rudder, and two propeller blades were smashed in. A sheet of ice had rammed a hole in her bottom.

"She's a sad sight, Commander," said Bartlett. "She may never make it home this year."

Peary's mouth tightened.

"We have got to get her back home, Captain."

"But you're worn out. Why the rush?"

"She needs repair work at once."

"Can't that wait?"

"I'm afraid not," said Peary. "We are going to come again next year!"

"I should have thought he wouldn't have wanted ever to see that place again," Bartlett wrote. *"But it was like him when he was lowest to be still planning for the future. Already he was thinking of his next attack on the Pole."*

No time was lost in starting back to the United States. During the next six weeks, however, the crip-

pled *Roosevelt* made little headway in ice-clogged Robeson and Kennedy Channels. The temperature dropped suddenly. New ice, six inches thick, closed in on the ship.

Unless the ship kept moving, she would be trapped again for months.

"We can't break through," Bartlett said to Peary one morning in mid-September 1906. "We're hardly moving—and I don't suppose there's much we can do about it."

Peary leaned over the rail and studied the ice. His memory mirrored his first Arctic voyage, when ice placed the *Eagle* in danger twenty years ago.

"We can try something," Peary said.

"What's that?"

"Have the crew smash the ice to open a water lane as we move along."

"Let's try it! What do the men do?"

Peary explained the trick he had learned from Captain Jackman of the *Eagle*. Bartlett ordered all sails set full. Then he called every man on deck, except those in the boiler room. The crew and the Eskimos going back to Greenland lined up on one side of the ship. Ice cracked sharply as the ship tipped to that side. The men raced across the deck. Again the ship leaned over and split the sheets of ice.

"Feed the boilers hard!" Bartlett roared at the men below. "Give her everything you've got."

Back and forth across the deck raced the men. The *Roosevelt* inched through the broken ice. A fast easterly breeze sprang up, speeding the ship along.

The *Roosevelt* was free again.

She stopped at Etah, Greenland, to let off the Eskimo families, then headed south. From October until December the badly battered ship sailed across rough seas. She reached New York City on Christmas Eve, 1906. Peary and his happy family were together again at a joyous time.

During the next three months Peary gave talks and wrote a book, *Nearest the Pole*, to help raise money for another expedition to the North Pole.

On March 30, 1907, the Peary Arctic Club announced that it would support "Commander Peary for a final attempt to reach the North Pole."

Peary hoped to set out on his eighth expedition to the Arctic in the summer of 1907. By that time he was sure all repair work on the crippled *Roosevelt* would be done. Repairs, however, dragged on and on.

Finally the big day came—July 6, 1908. The overhauled *Roosevelt* was ready to sail for Ellesmere Island from New York City.

Before leaving, Peary received thousands of friendly letters from Americans. One of his most eager admirers was President Theodore Roosevelt.

On July 6, he and Mrs. Roosevelt invited Peary and Josephine to a farewell lunch at the President's home on Sagamore Hill at Oyster Bay, N.Y.

After lunch, President Roosevelt visited the expedition ship. For an hour he inspected her decks, living quarters, engine rooms.

"Give it a good show this time, men," the President said. "Let this be a bully expedition all Americans will remember."

Peary was greatly touched by the President's confidence and well wishes. Just before President Roosevelt left the ship, Peary said to him:

"Mr. President, I shall put into this effort everything there is in me."

President Roosevelt took Peary's hand, shook it warmly, and answered:

"I believe in you, Peary, and I believe in your success—if it is within the possibility of man."

Later Peary expressed his feeling for Josephine:

"Another farewell, and there had been so many! Brave, noble, little woman! You have borne with me the brunt of all my Arctic work. The life is a dog's life, but the work is a man's work. . . . Should I succeed? . . . Should I return?"

CHAPTER TEN

REACHING THE POLE

"Rip 'em, Teddy! Bite 'em in two! Go it . . . that's fine my beauty! Rip 'em hard, Teddy."

Captain Bartlett sang out these words daily in August 1908. Throughout the month, he served as a lookout high in the crow's nest, a wooden barrel with the lid off. In the rigging just below the crow's nest, Peary clung to a narrow rope ladder.

Both men, calling out changes in course to the wheelsman, directed the *Roosevelt* through ice-packed Arctic waters. Slowly she slammed northward through Kane Basin, Kennedy Channel, Robeson Channel.

"It was a glorious battle," wrote Peary, "this charging of the ship against man's coldest enemy."

The *Roosevelt*, he reported, was kicked about by the floes as if she had been a football. "Imagine about 350 miles of almost solid ice—ice of all shapes and sizes, mountainous ice, flat ice, ragged and tortured ice. . . . *Rip! bang! boom!* The ship shook like a dish of jelly. . . ."

CAPTAIN BARTLETT

Peary's long experience in Arctic waters resulted in a quick early victory. Early in September, the *Roosevelt* reached Cape Sheridan at the northeast corner of Ellesmere Island.

She had fought her way to latitude 82 degrees 30 minutes north. This was a new record—the farthest north a ship ever had gone under her own power. Thanks to the *Roosevelt*, the expedition was fresh and strong for the march to the Pole. It lay at latitude 90 degrees, about 450 miles to the north.

Peary, however, did not plan to head north from Cape Sheridan.

"We'll first set up a base camp at Cape Columbia," he told the men.

"But that's a 90-mile sledge march to the northwest," protested Captain Bartlett. "Why go there?"

"When we move north on the Arctic Ocean its ice will be drifting to the east," Peary explained. "We might get to the Pole from here—but we'd never get back. By leaving from Cape Columbia, ninety miles to the west, we'll allow for the eastward ice drift."

"That's right," put in Henson. "Drifting ice could carry us clear past Greenland. We'd be out in the middle of nowhere!"

By the first week in September, ice held the *Roosevelt* fast at Cape Sheridan. Crowded aboard ship were Peary's seven-man expedition, the fifteen men of the crew, and forty-nine Eskimos. The Eskimos had come aboard at Etah, Greenland. As soon as the cargo was removed, Peary sent out hunting parties for musk oxen, polar bears, walrus, deer, hare, fish.

Meanwhile, an igloo camp was set up on shore at Cape Sheridan.

Peary, lonely for his family, surprised everyone on September 12, 1908. On that day, Marie Ahnighito was fifteen years old—so Peary held a birthday party in honor of his daughter. Every flag aboard the *Roosevelt* was flown. The ship cook made a huge cake decorated with bright icing and fifteen candles. The entire camp joined in with Peary to sing "Happy birthday, dear Marie Ahnighito . . ." to a girl three thousand miles away.

Four days later, the first group of men and dogs began sledging supplies by relays to Cape Columbia. All through the fall and winter Peary kept the men and the Eskimo families busy preparing for the trip to the Pole. The men trained dogs, prepared pemmican, stored food. They built new, extra-long 13-foot sledges, which could carry up to a thousand pounds of supplies. The Eskimo women sewed fur clothing, repaired boots, made harness straps.

By the end of February 1909, thousands of pounds of food and equipment were moved northwest to Cape Columbia.

At this jumping-off base with Peary were his six explorers, 17 Eskimos, 133 dogs, and 19 sledges. Of the six-man team three—Henson, Bartlett, and Ross G. Marvin—had served with Peary in the Arctic.

The other three were: Donald B. MacMillan, a high school teacher; Dr. J. W. Goodsell, the expedition doctor; George Borup, a young photographer.

All eyes were now turned to the north—and the Pole.

One evening Peary called his six-man team together. He explained how he hoped to reach the Pole with their help.

"We'll travel in six small units," Peary said. "Bartlett's group will break trail. Behind them will follow four support groups led by Dr. Goodsell, MacMillan, Borup, and Marvin."

"Just what do we do?" asked Dr. Goodsell.

"Each support group leader and his Eskimos keep the trail open. You also haul and bury extra food supplies for the main unit. I will lead the main party, which will have Henson and four Eskimos."

"Will all of us advance to the Pole?"

"I'm afraid not," Peary said. "Each support group will turn back for land after bringing up its supply sledge. In that way, we'll have fewer mouths to feed—and fewer men to worry about."

"How far from the Pole is Cape Columbia?" Borup asked.

"We are now about 413 miles from the Pole," said Peary. "I'm sure I can reach it if there are no delays. But we've got to move fast before the ice melts and cuts us off from land."

In fifty-below-zero weather on February 28, 1909,

the push to the Pole began. Bartlett's pioneer party headed due north from Cape Columbia.

Just before Peary moved out across the ice, he pulled out Josephine's American flag—now almost eleven years old. Peary wrapped it around his waist.

Peary's unit broke camp in the early morning of March 1. For three days the weather turned terribly cold, and rough winds shook up every unit. On March 4 the weather eased up. As the temperature rose, the ice began to melt. Blocking the men was a long lead of black water. Peary called it the "Hudson River."

By March 6 the lead widened. This gloomy day brightened somewhat for Peary when the sun appeared again for the first time in five months. The expedition, however, had been stopped.

Peary could do nothing but wait for the lead to freeze again. Or was this the beginning of the end? Delayed too long at any one place, Peary would never reach the Pole.

Stove fuel began to run low. Marvin and Borup were sent back to Cape Columbia for a fresh supply.

Their orders: "Rush back—and pick up our trail."

On March 11, the "Hudson River" lead began to close. Marvin and Borup were still not back with the needed fuel. Peary decided to push forward. He left this message for them in an igloo:

"Have waited here six days. Can wait no longer. We are short of fuel. Push on with all possible speed to overtake us."

With Bartlett and his Eskimos as pathfinders, the small units pressed northward.

On March 14, Marvin and Borup caught up with Peary and delivered the fuel. Peary realized that the time had come to streamline the expedition. Dr. Goodsell was sent back to Cape Columbia with two Eskimos, one sledge, and twelve dogs.

The next day MacMillan, one heel badly frozen, went back with two Eskimos, two sledges, fourteen dogs. That same afternoon, thunderous booms rolled across the sea ice. The steady rumbling worried Peary.

"I don't like the sound of that," he told the men. "It's not a storm. Ice is splitting up ahead and forming leads."

"I hope they freeze over again before we get to them," said Bartlett. "We've had our fill of delays."

Within hours the men reached a series of long, wide cracks. Floating sheets of ice, some 100 feet wide, bobbed in the black water.

"We can't wait here," Peary said. "The sea is moving too fast for the ice to freeze hard."

"But how can we cross?"

"There's only one quick way. Jump onto a passing chunk and load up on it. Then use it as a raft to get to the next chunk—until you reach the other shore. Borup, you'll have to be very careful."

This was a reminder that most of the food supplies—500 pounds—were on Borup's sledge.

All units—except Borup's—easily "ferried" on ice

rafts to the opposite shore. Borup had no trouble until he was almost there. Two pieces of floating ice separated just as Borup's dog team was crossing. One by one the helpless dogs slipped into the water.

The sledge slid to the edge of the ice.

Borup, alone on the ice raft, grabbed the end of the heavy sledge. Using every ounce of his strength, he stopped it from going over the edge. Then, with one hand, he reached into the water, seized the harness of the dog nearest him, and lifted it on the ice. This pulled the next dog back to the edge of the ice. Borup kept yanking and lifting the harness straps until all the dogs were saved.

For the next few days, the men pushed northward in fifty-below-zero-weather. On March 19, Peary reduced the party by sending back Borup with three Eskimos, one sledge, and sixteen dogs.

A week later, the men stood at 86 degrees 38 minutes. Peary asked Ross Marvin to return with two Eskimos, one sledge, seventeen dogs.

"Be careful of the leads, my boy," were Peary's last words to Marvin. Peary never again saw Marvin, who was to lose his life on this return march.

On March 28, Peary broke his own "farthest-north" record of 87 degrees, 6 minutes, which he had set in 1906.

For several days leads opened up all around the men, but they floated across safely on ice rafts. Worn out, Peary drove himself forward. On April 1, with food running low, he asked Bartlett to return with two Eskimos, one sledge, and eighteen dogs.

Bartlett hated to leave. Yet he agreed that Peary was right in sending him back instead of Henson. Bartlett was the only man who could handle the *Roosevelt* and get the expedition home.

The final dash for the Pole—130 miles away—was now to begin. With Peary were Henson, four Eskimos, and forty dogs.

They pressed to the north at top speed, never sleeping more than a few hours between long marches. The temperature—not too cold—and the ice—not too soft—were perfect for fast travel. The men averaged thirty miles a day.

"Give me three more days of this weather!" Peary begged in his diary.

By April 4 he was close to 89 degrees north latitude.

A little before midnight on April 5 some thirty-five miles from the Pole—the men started out on what Peary hoped would be THE victory march. By noon they had advanced to 89 degrees 57 minutes.

They were three miles away! Peary wrote:

"The Pole at last. The prize of three centuries. My dream and goal for twenty years. Mine at last! I cannot bring myself to realize it. It all seems so simple. . . ."

On the morning of April 6, 1909, the men covered the last few miles.

Robert E. Peary had reached the North Pole.

CHAPTER ELEVEN

"I RETURN MY GREATEST TREASURE"

THE North Pole!—the only place on Earth where every step in any direction is toward the south.

Peary's instruments could not show him the Pole's exact position. And when clouds appeared they were

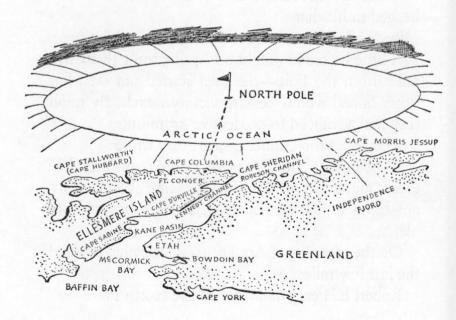

useless. So he continued forward a few miles until the sun broke through. Then he made an exact reading. He had passed the Pole!

"It seemed hard to realize that on the first mile of the march, I had been going north," he wrote, "and on the last—*though still traveling ahead in the same direction*—I was going south. In order to return to my camp, I must turn and go north again, and then, still keeping on in a straight line, go south!"

Peary, Henson, and the four Eskimos now began moving back and forth over several miles in a crisscross pattern. At some point in these short marches, Peary knew he had stood squarely on the Pole "where north and south and east and west blend into one."

After a careful series of checks, Peary asked the Eskimos to build a high pile of ice blocks. When they finished, Peary opened his fur suit and slipped Josephine's flag from his waist. For a moment he stared at the tattered "Stars and Stripes, the silk flag which I had carried for so many years wrapped around my body on all my later Arctic journeys."

Peary turned to Henson.

"Plant the Stars and Stripes at the very top of the mound, Matt—at the North Pole."

Henson fastened the flag to a tall stick and hammered it into the highest ice block.

Peary's long-sought moment of victory was at hand.

"As I watched the flag fluttering in the crisp air of the Pole, I thought of the 23 years of my own life

which had been spent in laboring toward that goal. I realized that at last I had made good," he wrote.

Peary also had made good his promise to Josephine to fly her gift at the Pole. He saluted the flag.

Henson, moved by this scene, had the four Eskimos join him in giving three loud cheers. Then he ran over to Peary.

"Let me be the first to congratulate you, sir, on the discovery of the North Pole."

After taking several photographs of the flag, Peary brought it down again. He cut a strip out of it, from an upper corner to the far lower corner. Then he rolled this strip and put it in a bottle with two messages. They were, in part:

"90 North Latitude, North Pole, April 6, 1909. Arrived here today, 27 marches from Cape Columbia. I have with me five men . . ."

"90 North Latitude, North Pole, April 6, 1909. I have today hoisted the national ensign of the United States of America at this place, which my observations indicate to be the North Polar axis. . . ."

Peary buried the bottle in the ice.

The men remained at the Pole for thirty hours. Peary made sun studies, checked ice forms, kept records of changes in temperature.

Now came the dash for home. Peary turned to have one last look at the Pole. A sad feeling weighed on Peary as he realized "this scene my eyes will never see again."

He walked to Henson and said: "Let's go home, Matt, let's go home."

Off they sped—but not for long.

Five miles from the Pole, Peary noticed a deep crack in the ice. He stopped and asked the Eskimos to chop through the ice with pickaxes until they hit water. Peary removed a large spool from one of the sledges. Wrapped around the spool were 9,000 feet of fine piano wire. Henson tied a heavy weight to the end of the wire and dropped it into the water.

The weight did not touch bottom. This was proof —the first of its kind—that the North Pole and its surrounding area lay in a vast and deep ice-covered sea.

"We've made an important finding, Matt," Peary said. "The North Pole is definitely located in the sea—not on a land mass."

On the first day's return to Ellesmere Island, the men covered thirty-five miles. Speed was vital, for the ice around them showed signs of breaking up in the spring thaw. Strong spring tides might then set them adrift and keep them from reaching shore.

Day after day they hurried on . . . now battling a sudden blizzard . . . now floating on ice rafts across wide leads . . . now climbing over piled-up ice ridges. In Peary's words it was "big travel, small sleep, hustle every minute."

As supplies began to run low, they killed the weakest dogs for food. Hunger drove them on against strong winds that kicked snow in their faces—"stinging like needles."

In mid-April the weather improved, but they lost the main trail. A series of wide leads and steady winds had scattered it about. Peary pioneered the party, found the trail again, and stuck with it.

A few hours before midnight, on April 22, they left the polar sea and stepped on land again. They had covered more than 400 miles in only sixteen days.

"I thought my Eskimos had gone crazy," wrote Peary. "They yelled and called and danced until they fell from utter exhaustion. As Ootah sank on his sledge he remarked in Eskimo: 'The devil is asleep or having trouble with his wife or we should never have come back so easily'."

As they neared the ship, Captain Bartlett leaned over a rail to greet them. He was shocked by what he saw. These were shadows of the men he left on April 1, when he had turned back from the polar ice.

Their bodies were thin, their shoulders droopy. Each man had a wrinkled, strained look to his face. Their eyes were dull and half-shut.

Peary looked the worst. He had lost at least thirty pounds in the last six weeks. He could hardly walk. He moved slowly, dragging and scraping his feet along in pain. His lips were pressed together, forming a tight line across his bony face.

Bartlett had bad news to report: Ross Marvin died during his return march. This shocked and saddened

Peary, who was fond of Marvin. He was the first man
—in twenty-three years—to have lost his life while
serving under Peary in the Arctic.

After twelve hours of sound sleep, Peary called
Bartlett into his cabin.

"Have all the Eskimos report on deck immediately,
Captain," Peary said.

Bartlett rounded them up in short order. Then, for
having done their jobs so well for the expedition,

Peary gave each man, woman, and child a choice of gifts: knives, hatchets, telescopes, rifles, bullets, stoves, beads, mirrors, and so on.

The four Eskimos who reached the North Pole with Peary received whaleboats, tents, binoculars, and other "treasures."

On July 18 the ice in Cape Sheridan began to break up. In September the ship pulled into Indian Harbor off the coast of Labrador. This gave Peary his first chance to report news of the expedition directly to the United States.

His first telegram, sent out on September 5, 1909, went to Josephine.

"Have made good at last. I have the Pole. Am well. Love. Bert."

The next wire was to the Associated Press, a news agency:

"Stars and Stripes nailed to the North Pole—Peary."

For the next two weeks the *Roosevelt* had clear sailing. She sped south past Labrador and Newfoundland, then turned southwest toward Nova Scotia's Cape Breton Island.

Small brightly decorated boats, sounding their horns wildly, came out to give Peary a royal welcome. The *Roosevelt* soon neared the small town of Sydney on Cape Breton. Crowds of cheering Canadians lined the edge of the water front.

Peary was delighted to see a trim white boat pull

up alongside the *Roosevelt.* Shouting to him from the deck were Josephine, Marie Ahnighito, and Robert Edwin, Jr.

Within the next few minutes Peary and his family were together again after nearly fifteen months.

Within the next week the family was at home on Eagle Island in Maine. One evening Peary told Josephine that he had something for her.

"What is it, Bert? A surprise?"

"It's not really a gift for it has always been yours."

He unwrapped a flat package and lifted out an American flag—his polar flag.

"This is the first and only national flag to fly at the North Pole," Peary said. "I want you to have it."

He handed the tattered silk remains to her.

"Once it was your gift to me," Peary said. "It has always been my greatest treasure. Now I return it."

Peary put his arm around Josephine.

"Neither the flag nor I would ever have gotten there if it hadn't been for you," he said. "I hope you will feel that the flag has been used worthily and that I have added some glory to it."

"You have, for all time, for yourself and for the nation," said Josephine.

America was never to forget Peary as one of her greatest explorers.

"I recommend fitting recognition by Congress of the great achievement of Robert E. Peary," said President William Howard Taft in 1910. Soon after, Congress approved this vote of thanks: "Be it enacted . . . that the Thanks of Congress be tendered to Robert E. Peary, United States Navy, for his Arctic Explorations resulting in reaching the North Pole."

And in less than a month Peary was promoted to the rank of rear admiral in the United States Navy.

CHAPTER TWELVE

HONORED AMERICAN

Peary, Godspeed! . . .
A brave man dares again.
—RICHARD LE GALLIENNE

FEW explorers showed as much determination and courage as Peary. His name long will appear on the list of America's heroes.

"Peary has performed one of the great feats of our time," wrote President Theodore Roosevelt. "He has won high honor for himself and for his country."

Peary's honors were many:

Geographers and scientists around the world rated him as one of the greatest explorers of all time.

Some thirty medals, trophies, honorary degrees were awarded to him by foreign governments, scientific societies, universities.

The farthest-north land region of the world, in northern Greenland, was named for him: Peary Land.

A United States warship was christened *Peary* in his memory.

And one of the most satisfying honors: Expedition

members and Eskimos who worked with Peary had only praise for his leadership.

Said Matt Henson . . . "He was a man among men, a proud iron man. Peary could have gotten me to go to the end of the world with him."

Captain Robert A. Bartlett . . . "Thank heaven it was my privilege to serve under such a man, to be so close to him. . . . The Eskimos loved him."

Donald B. MacMillan . . . "He knew how to handle men and never had need to give an order directly. He might say 'I would like to have you do this,' or 'Today when you get a chance,' or 'Let's see if we can finish this morning.'"

George Borup . . . "What a leader to serve under! Always kind, considerate. Always giving us good advice, going out of his way to help us. He never knew when he was licked. He always could encourage us and hold all of us together."

Peary gathered useful information about Arctic weather, mineral resources, ice flows, tides, geography, animal life, Eskimos, huskies, atmospheric pressure, glaciers, sea depths.

"Peary's discovery that the Arctic Ocean was more than 9,000 feet deep permitted us to consider a trip under the ice," reported United States Commander William R. Anderson, skipper of the *Nautilus*. Under his command the *Nautilus*, America's first atompowered submarine, made the first crossing under the North Pole. The date: August 3, 1958.

No one battled against the Arctic as long or as hard as Peary.

Thanks to him, polar travel methods were greatly improved. He learned to respect and make use of Eskimo skills, clothing, equipment, dogs. He learned how to protect himself and his men against cold and hunger, how to keep them busy and fit during the long Arctic winter. He learned when to start an expedition and when to end it, when to use a large party and when to use a small one.

After conquering the North Pole, Peary turned to aviation. He became one of the nation's most eager air pioneers and prophets. "He who commands the air commands all," he warned Americans.

Admiral Peary died on February 20, 1920, in Washington, D.C. He was buried with full naval honors at Arlington National Cemetery.

In 1922 a memorial ceremony was held at his grave. Taking part were President Warren G. Harding, high-ranking members of his Cabinet, United States military leaders, leading foreign officials.

All came to pay their respects to Admiral Peary and to a white granite monument built in his honor. The monument, shaped like a globe, represents the Earth and shows the continents in outline. A bronze star marks the location of the North Pole. One side of the base bears Admiral Peary's life motto:

"Inveniam viam aut faciam" . . .

"I shall find a way or make one."

ROBERT E. PEARY